Route Rec

D1549801

SOUTHERN
REGION

Colin J. Marsden

LONDON

IAN ALLAN LTD

First published 1985

ISBN 0 7110 1553 8

© Ian Allan Ltd 1985

Published by Ian Allan Ltd, Shepperton, Surrey; and printed by Ian Allan Printing Ltd at their works at Coombelands in Runnymede, England.

Rear Cover:
Traversing the 2.51-mile single line section between Brading and Smallbrook Junction a seven-car formation with spare car No 10 leading, heads the 11.02 Shanklin-Ryde of 13 June 1982. *Colin J. Marsden*

Cover:
The 14.35 Waterloo-Weymouth is seen at Northam Junction on 19 August 1983. *Colin J. Marsden*

Above:
A 12-car CIG/VEP/CIG formation traverses the quadruple tracks of the SWD main line between Walton-on-Thames and Weybridge on 14 May 1980 with a fast Portsmouth Harbour-Waterloo service. *Colin J. Marsden*

Introduction

Welcome to *Route Recognition No 1 – Southern Region.* This product contained in the now well established Recognition format takes the reader over all lines covered by the SR operating authority.

For reasons of clarity, the product is divided into three main sections: 1) South Western Division [SWD], 2) Central Division [CD] and 3) South Eastern Division [SED]. Each of these Divisions are then divided into separate routes 26 for the SWD, 17 for the CD and 16 for the SED. These are again broken down into sections for a detailed description. Each of these short route sections are usually of about 10-20 miles in length and normally allocated one page. At the top of the page is a short technical description of the route/section covered on that page, whilst at the bottom of the page is a straight line map (not to scale) giving the between station mileage (in decimal miles) and junction positions, thus giving at a glance recognition of the track section covered. In the centre of the page a photograph shows a train on part of the line covered with an extended caption, emphasis being given to the places on the route rather than the photographic subject. Where there are junctions, a route key is given helping the reader or traveller to follow the progression of his journey. At junctions, mileages to the nearest station are quoted. There are maps both at the front and back of this book covering the main and suburban lines, detailed with the section numbers for easy reference.

It is hoped that readers of *Route Recognition – SR* will find it a useful guide to the lines of Southern Region.

I would like to record my thanks to the many railway staff who have provided assistance with this project, especially the Public Affairs office at Waterloo. Thanks are also due to Mr J. N. Faulkner, who provided and checked much of the heading data, and Mrs Jean Marsden who has undertaken the unenviable task of typing the manuscript.

Colin J. Marsden
Surbiton
June 1985

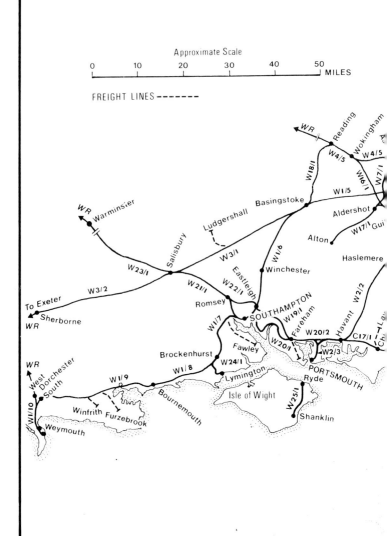

Approximate Scale

| 0 | 10 | 20 | 30 | 40 | 50 |
| MILES |

FREIGHT LINES -------

WR
Reading
Wokingham
W4/5
W4/5
W18/1
W16/1
W7/1
W1/5
Aldershot
WR
Warminster
Basingstoke
W17/1 Gui
Ludgershall
Alton
W3/1
W1/6
Haslemere
Salisbury
W23/1
Eastleigh
Winchester
W3/2
W21/1
W2/2
To Exeter
W22/1
Sherborne
Romsey
SOUTHAMPTON
W19/1
WR
W1/7
Fareham
Havant
W2/3
C17/1
La
Ch
W20/2
WR
West
Dorchester
Brockenhurst
Fawley
W20/1
PORTSMOUTH
South
W1/8
W24/1
W1/9
Lymington
Ryde
W1/10
Winfrith Furzebrook
Bournemouth
Isle of Wight
W25/1
Weymouth
Shanklin

4

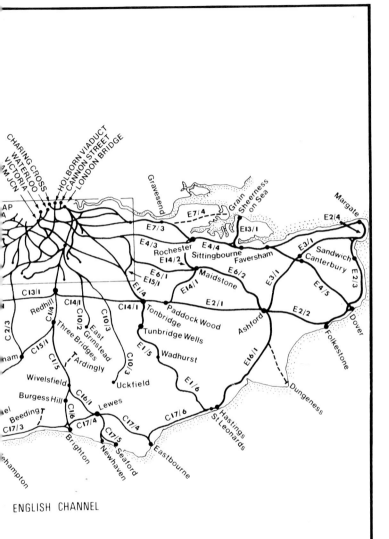

CHARING CROSS
WATERLOO
VICTORIA
...M JCN
HOLBORN VIADUCT
CANNON STREET
LONDON BRIDGE
...AP

Gravesend

Grain
Sheerness on Sea
Margate

E7/4
E7/3
E4/4
E13/1
E2/4
E4/3
Rochester
Sittingbourne
Faversham
E3/1
Sandwich
Canterbury
E2/3
E14/2
E6/2
E3/1
E6/1
Maidstone
E15/1
E14/1
E4/5
E1/4
E2/1
C13/1
Paddock Wood
Ashford
E2/2
Redhill
C14/1
C14/1
Tonbridge
Dover
C2/3
C14/1
C10/2
C10/3
Tunbridge Wells
Folkestone
C15/1
Three Bridges
East Grinstead
E1/5
Wadhurst
E16/1
...nam
C11/5
Ardingly
C10/3
Wivelsfield
Uckfield
E1/6
Burgess Hill
C16/1
Lewes
Dungeness
...el
Beeding
C16/1
C17/3
C16/1
C17/4
C17/4
C17/6
Hastings
St Leonards
Brighton
Seaford
Eastbourne
...ehampton
Newhaven
C17/5

ENGLISH CHANNEL

5

Route: W1
WATERLOO-WEYMOUTH

Section: W1/1 Waterloo-Clapham Junction

Number of lines: 8
Signalling type: Colour light
Constructed by: LSWR
Year opened: 1839
(Waterloo-Nine Elms 1848)
Services: Passenger
Types of traction: EMU,
DMU, Loco-hauled
Electrified: Yes

Notes: Occasional
freight/departmental traffic.

Large shunting and stabling
yard situated between Main
and Windsor lines at
Clapham Junction.

The 3.9-mile section from Waterloo to Clapham Junction has the highest
concentration of trains approaching any of the London termini and indeed of
any BR tracks in the country. A total of eight running lines are available for
services, which are divided into three sections – local lines, main lines and
the Windsor lines. Departing from Vauxhall on the down local, Class 455/8 No
5802 forms a rush-hour service to Guildford via Cobham.
Colin J. Marsden

Route: W1
WATERLOO-WEYMOUTH

Section: W1/2 Clapham Junction-New Malden

Number of lines: 4
Signalling type: Colour light
Constructed by: LSWR
Year opened: 1839
Services: Passenger
Types of traction: EMU,
DMU, Loco-hauled
Electrified: Yes

Notes: Occasional
freight/departmental traffic.

Sizeable EMU depot situated
at East Wimbledon, large
variety of types usually
visible in area.

From Clapham Junction, where the Windsor lines diverge, the main route
continues as a four track section as far as Worting Junction (Basingstoke). As
the line progresses several branches diverge at Wimbledon and Raynes Park,
these being fed by surburban line services. Most passenger services on this
section are EMU operated except for Waterloo-Salisbury-Exeter duties and
infrequent trains to and from Southampton Docks or Weymouth Quay, which
are locomotive operated. Little freight traffic traverses these lines except for a
few daily vans trains between the coast and Clapham Junction, and coal
traffic for the Chessington line. Two Class 73s Nos 73.102/125 approach
Raynes Park on 24 April 1984 with a Southampton-Clapham Junction empty
vans train. *Colin J. Marsden*

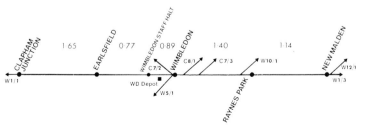

Route: W1
WATERLOO-WEYMOUTH

Section: W1/3 New Malden-Weybridge

Number of lines: 4
Signalling type: Colour light
Constructed by: LSWR
Year opened: 1839
Services: Passenger

Types of traction: EMU, DMU, Loco-hauled
Electrified: Yes
Notes: Occasional freight/departmental traffic.

At New Malden the line to Kingston diverges from the main line, which then proceeds on to Berrylands and Surbiton, where 1-mile after the station the lines to Hampton Court and Guildford via Effingham Junction separate at Hampton Court Junction, the main route continuing to Weybridge. Surbiton station rebuilt to typical SR style in the mid-1930s has two island platforms with faces on both up main and local track, and the down local and loop line. Berrylands, Hersham and Weybridge stations have only side platforms whereas others have centre island platforms as well, feeding the main lines but these are not used for regular service. At Weybridge the branch diverges to Addlestone and Staines. A Class 412 No 2303 passes Surbiton with a Portsmouth-Waterloo train on 16 April 1984 while a 4VEP awaits the signal to cross from the down main into the down local platform road.
Colin J. Marsden

Route: W1
WATERLOO-WEYMOUTH

Section: W1/4 Weybridge-Woking

Number of lines: 4
Signalling type: Colour light
Constructed by: LSWR
Year opened: 1839
Services: Passenger, freight

Types of traction: EMU, DMU, Loco-hauled
Electrified: Yes

The four track main line continues throughout this section. 0.11-miles on the London side of Byfleet & New Haw station lays Byfleet Junction where a connection exists to the Weybridge-Addlestone line. This spur is normally used only by freight traffic but is passed for passenger operation. At West Byfleet station both down local and main lines have platform faces, whereas only the local track on the up side has platform facilities. The route then continues on to Woking where there are platforms for all lines; there is also a four-car down facing bay platform. Traffic over this section is usually formed of EMUs on passenger services with infrequent locomotive hauled duties on Waterloo-Salisbury-Exeter services. However at Woking sizeable civil engineering yards exist on both sides of the line which see a number of freight/departmental trains. The section from Byfleet junction to Woking also sees a number of inter-regional freight services emanating from ER/LMR. Class 50 No 50.005 *Collingwood* passes West Byfleet on 20 April 1984 with the 11.10 Waterloo-Exeter service. *Colin J. Marsden*

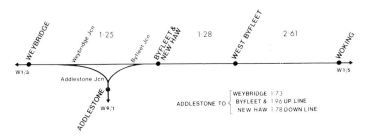

9

Route: W1
WATERLOO-WEYMOUTH

Section: W1/5 Woking-Basingstoke

Number of lines: 4
Signalling type: Colour light
Constructed by: LSWR
Year opened: 1839
Services: Passenger, freight
Types of traction: EMU,

DMU, Loco-hauled
Electrified: Yes
Notes: Large permanent way yards at Woking, hosting a wide variety of rolling stock and traction types.

A short distance south of Woking is Woking Junction where the Guildford and Portsmouth line parts from the main arterial route which continues throughout this section as a four track line with only two divergencies – one at Pirbright Junction 1.50-miles on the country side of Brookwood, serving the line to Aldershot and Alton; and the other the London side of Basingstoke where the line to Reading joins in. All intermediate passenger stations on this section have platform facilities on local lines only. There is a sizeable station at Basingstoke with platform facilities on all lines; there are also up and down bay platforms. Both passenger and freight services regularly traverse these tracks, EMUs normally being used on passenger diagrams. The Reading line joining in at Basingstoke brings a sizeable amount of freight traffic to the SR including a number of freightliner trains. A REP/TC/TC formation passes Newnham, near Basingstoke, on 13 April 1984 with the 09.00 Bournemouth-Waterloo train. *Colin J. Marsden*

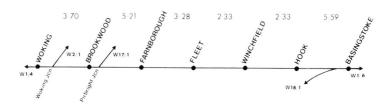

Route: W1
WATERLOO-WEYMOUTH

Section: W1/6 Basingstoke-Southampton

Number of lines: See Notes
Signalling type: Colour light
Constructed by: LSWR
Year opened: 1840
Services: Passenger, freight
Types of traction: EMU, DMU, Loco-hauled
Electrified: Yes

Large permanent way and marshalling yards exist at Eastleigh where a wide variety of rolling stock and traction types can be seen.

Notes: Basingstoke-Worting Junction – 4 track. Worting Junction-Shawford – 2 track. Shawford-Eastleigh – 4 track. Eastleigh-St Denys – 2 track. St Denys-Northam Junction – 4 track. Northam Junction-Southampton – 2 track.

The four track section of the SWD continues on from Basingstoke to Worting Junction, 2.5-miles to the west, where the twin non-electrified route to Salisbury diverges. The main line, predominantly twin-tracked, continues to Southampton, with additional running lines, as noted in the heading. From Worting Junction the main line continues the 7.80 miles to Micheldever where an oil siding is to be found on the down side. After a further 8.43 miles Winchester is reached which is served by semi-fast and stopping trains between Waterloo and Bournemouth. In the Eastleigh area additional up and down running lines are provided which assist with additional traffic generated by sizeable yards to the London end of the station. Directly at the London end of the station the non-electrified line from Romsey joins the route, while at the country end the line to Fareham diverges. Directly after this the entrances to Eastleigh Works and the diesel depot are situated. The route carries on to Southampton Airport, Swaythling and St Denys where the non-electrified line from Fareham joins. The route then becomes a four track section for the short distance to Northam Junction where the main line (2 tracks) bears off to the right into Southampton and a straight route continues into Southampton Docks. Both EMU/DMU and locomotive hauled passenger trains, together with a notable amount of freight, operate in this area.

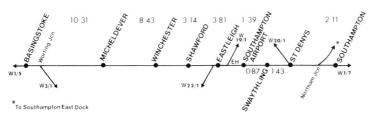

* To Southampton East Dock

4TC No 408 approaches Northam Junction on 12 April 1984 with a Waterloo-Bournemouth semi-fast service. *Colin J. Marsden*

Route: W1
WATERLOO-WEYMOUTH

Section: W1/7 Southampton-Brockenhurst

Number of lines: See Notes

Signalling type: Colour light

Constructed by: LSWR

Year opened: 1847

Services: Passenger, freight

Types of traction: EMU, DMU, Loco-hauled

Electrified: Yes

Notes:

Southampton-Millbrook
— 4 track.

Millbrook-Brockenhurst
— 2 track.

The section on to Brockenhurst is basically two tracked with two additional running lines between Southampton and Millbrook, where another line diverges into Southampton Docks. At the country end of Redbridge station the twin non-electrified route to Romsey diverges to the right. Soon after Totton station the freight only branch to Fawley veers off to the left which is the host of several daily oil trains to and from various parts of the country. The twin main line continues to Brockenhurst with intermediate stations at Lyndhurst Road and Beaulieu Road. Class 47 No 47.489 approaches Beaulieu Road on 12 April 1984 with a westbound inter-regional service to Poole. *Colin J. Marsden*

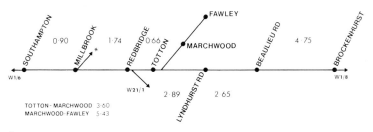

TOTTON - MARCHWOOD 3·60
MARCHWOOD-FAWLEY 5·43

*To Southampton West Dock

Route: W1
WATERLOO-WEYMOUTH

Section: W1/8 Brockenhurst-Bournemouth

Number of lines: 2
Signalling type: Colour light
Constructed by: LSWR
Year opened: 1888
Services: Passenger, freight
Types of traction: EMU,
Loco-hauled
Electrified: Yes

An additional line starts from Brockenhurst station running parallel with the main line to Lymington Junction where the line diverges to Lymington Pier. The double tracked main line continues on to Bournemouth with five intermediate stations, all of which have side platforms. Services on this portion of line consist of the hourly fast, semi-fast and stopping trains to Bournemouth punctuated infrequently by locomotive-hauled inter-regional traffic to and from the Midlands. Freight on this section has about half-a dozen diagrams but often not all operate. 4TC No 430 leads a 12-car formation towards Sway on 12 April 1984 with the 12.35 Waterloo-Weymouth train.   *Colin J. Marsden*

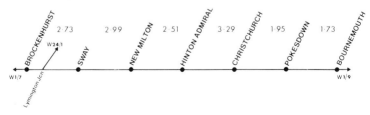

14

Route: W1
WATERLOO-WEYMOUTH

Section: W1/9 Bournemouth-Dorchester

Number of lines: $2^{\dagger}$
Signalling type: Semaphore, Colour light
Constructed by: LSWR
Year opened:
1874 Bournemouth-Poole,
1847 Hamworthy-Dorchester
Services: Passenger, freight
Types of traction: EMU, Loco-hauled
Electrified: See Notes
Notes: Electrified as far as Branksome, for access to BM depot.
† Single between Moreton and Dorchester.

Onwards from Bournemouth the electrified route only continues as far as Branksome, giving access via a reverse shunt to Bournemouth electric depot. The double track route continues as far as Moreton where a single line exists to a point near Dorchester South. Public service is provided hourly formed of portions from fast Waterloo-Bournemouth services, trains being formed of Class 33/1 locomotive and TC stock. Additional infrequent inter-regional services operate from the Midlands as far as Poole. Diverging from the route at Hamworthy is the 2.05-mile goods line to Poole Docks which sees occasional steel traffic. Another diversion from the main route is at Worgret Junction west of Wareham, where the 3.33-mile line to Furzebrook turns off to the left. Class 33/1 No 33.107 leads 4TC No 425 down Parkstone Bank towards the station in spring 1984. *Colin J. Marsden*

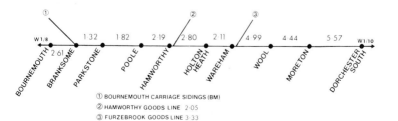

① BOURNEMOUTH CARRIAGE SIDINGS (BM)
② HAMWORTHY GOODS LINE 2·05
③ FURZEBROOK GOODS LINE 3·33

Route: W1
WATERLOO-WEYMOUTH

Section: W1/10 Dorchester-Weymouth

Number of lines: 2
Signalling type: Colour light, semaphore
Constructed by: GWR
Year opened: 1857
Services: Passenger, freight
Types of traction: Loco-hauled
Electrified: No

The remaining 6.88 miles from Dorchester to Weymouth passes through some of the most scenic countryside on the SR. A short distance beyond Dorchester South station is Dorchester West Junction where a single chord connection joins in from Dorchester West and the Yeovil Pen Mill line; westwards the lines serves Upwey and then Weymouth. 0.22-miles on the London side of Weymouth station is Weymouth Quay Junction where the single line to Weymouth Quay diverges. This 1.25-mile branch passes through the streets of Weymouth before terminating adjacent to the dock berth. Services over main sections are usually confined to the hourly London services operated by TC and Class 33/1 formations, supplemented by an infrequent DMMU service from Bristol/Westbury. A number of additional loco operated trains work on summer Saturdays to and from Weymouth running on both the WR line via Dorchester West and the SR main line. Trains to and from Weymouth Quay consist of two through services from Waterloo operated during the summer months only. Two 4TCs are propelled up Upwey bank on 5 September 1984 by Class 33/1 No 33.113 forming the 15.33 Weymouth-Waterloo service. *Colin J. Marsden*

Route: W2
WOKING-PORTSMOUTH
HARBOUR

Section: W2/1 Woking-Haslemere

Number of lines: 2
Signalling type: Colour light
Constructed by: LSWR
Year opened:
1845 (to Guildford),
1849 (to Godalming),
1859 (to Haslemere)
Services: Passenger
Types of traction: EMU,
Loco-hauled
Electrified: Yes

Notes: Occasional
freight/departmental traffic.

The second of the SWD main routes concerns the Portsmouth line which diverges from the Waterloo-Weymouth line at Woking Junction to the west of Woking station, and being a double track section. After departure from Woking the line passes through Worplesdon and on to Guildford where, just prior to the station, the routes from Effingham Junction and Ash converge. Guildford has a sizeable station with eight platforms. Onwards the line heads for Farncombe but 1.19-miles after Guildford at Shalford Junction the branch for Redhill goes off to the left. The main line continuing to Haslemere winds through some very splendid Surrey countryside, and all intermediate stations between Guildford and Haslemere have side platforms. An additional up loop line is provided at Haslemere and with the up main line signalled for reverse operation this provides a potential to run fast trains around stopping services. Most trains on this section are EMU operated except for a few inter-regional duties emulating from Portsmouth which are locomotive operated. DMUs traverse the section between Shalford Junction and Guildford. Class 412 No 2305 approaches Guildford with a fast Portsmouth Harbour-Waterloo service. *Colin J. Marsden*

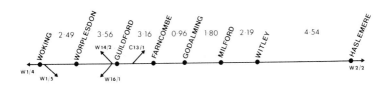

Route: W2
WOKING-PORTSMOUTH HARBOUR

Section: W2/2 Haslemere-Havant

Number of lines: 2
Signalling type: Colour light
Constructed by: LSWR
Year opened: 1859
Services: Passenger

Types of traction: EMU, Loco-hauled
Electrified: Yes
Notes: Occasional freight/departmental traffic.

The twin tracked Portsmouth line continues through this section to Havant where, at the London end of the station, the 'Coastway' line from Brighton joins it. All stations on this route with the exception of Havant, have side platforms only; Havant station having 'loop' platform lines with two centre tracks. Services traversing this route are usually confined to one fast, one semi-fast and one slow train in each direction per hour, all formed of EMU stock, a few loco operated services operate but amount to no more than two or three per day. A 12-car CIG/BIG/CIG formation forms a Waterloo-Portsmouth fast service near Liphook during 1982.
Colin J. Marsden

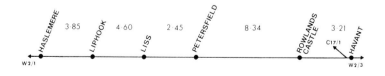

Route: W2
WOKING-PORTSMOUTH HARBOUR

Section: W2/3 Havant-Portsmouth Harbour

Number of lines: See Notes
Signalling type: Colour light
Constructed by: LSWR (Joint with LBSCR)
Year opened: 1847
Services: Passenger/freight
Types of traction: EMU, DMU, Loco-hauled
Electrified: Yes

Notes: Havant-Fratton – 2 track.
Fratton-Portsmouth & Southsea – 3 track (2Dn/1Up).
Portsmouth & Southsea – Portsmouth Harbour – 2 track.
Sizeable yard/depot situated on down side at Fratton.

The flow of traffic to the south of Havant is considerably increased by additional 'Coastway' services. After departing from Havant the double track continues to Fratton from where an additional down running line is added as far as Portsmouth & Southsea, the one-up/one-down continuing on to Portsmouth Harbour. 2.30 miles south of Bedhampton station a right-hand divergence leads to Cosham Junction and the Fareham line, and after a further 0.56-miles another junction is situated between the Fareham and Portsmouth line facing south. Services over this route are mainly formed of EMU stock, however diesel-hauled services operate between the WR, Southampton, Fareham and Portsmouth, thus providing a good variety of motive power between Hilsea and Portsmouth. The Cosham Junction-Havant section also sees an amount of locomotive-hauled freight traffic as most stone services for Central and South Eastern locations are routed via here. At Fratton there are sizeable yards, also an EMU depot and locomotive fuelling facility.

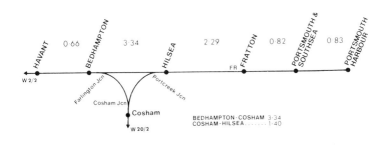

BEDHAMPTON-COSHAM 3·34
COSHAM-HILSEA....... 1·40

A Class 207 DEMU No 1315 heads for Fratton in the summer of 1984 with a Portsmouth Harbour-Reading service.
Colin J. Marsden

Route: W3
BASINGSTOKE-SHERBORNE

Section: W3/1 Worting Junction-Salisbury (including Luggershall Branch)

Number of lines: 2†
Signalling type: Colour light
Constructed by: LSWR
Year opened:
1854 (to Andover),
1857 (to Salisbury)
Services: Passenger, freight
Types of traction: DMU
Loco-hauled,
Electrified: No*

Notes: *Electrified between Basingstoke-Worting Junction.
† Luggershall branch – single line.

Diverging from the SWD main line at Worting Junction is the former LSWR main line to the west, now reduced to secondary status. The twin tracked non-electrified route passes through Overton and Whitchurch which both have short side platforms before reaching Andover, which is now only a shadow of its former self. Only side platforms now survive, with small yards mainly handling fertilizer and MoD traffic. After the line departs from Andover an additional line runs parallel for 1.60 miles as far as Redpost Junction where the line bears right and forms the single line to the Ministry of Defence at Ludgershall. The main line continues on past Grateley to Laverstock North junction where a connection is provided with the Romsey Line. Shortly after this another line converges from the left bringing the Romsey route into the main line at Tunnel Junction, the twin track line continuing on to Salisbury. Sizeable yards are provided in the immediate station area mainly dealing with stone traffic. Services on this line consist of the two hourly Waterloo-Exeter trains with intermediate semi-fast services terminating at Salisbury. Inter-regional trains from Portsmouth to Bristol traverse the section between Tunnel Junction and Salisbury. A moderate amount of freight traffic also operates, mainly in the Salisbury area.

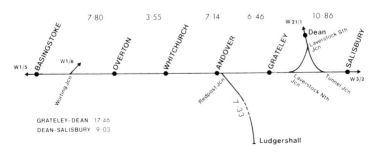

GRATELEY-DEAN 17·46
DEAN-SALISBURY 9·03

Class 50 No 50.008 *Thunderer* passes Whitchurch with the 09.38 Exeter-Waterloo on 13 April 1984. *Colin J. Marsden*

Route: W3
BASINGSTOKE-SHERBORNE

Section: W3/2 Salisbury-Sherborne

Number of lines: Note 1
Signalling type: Colour light
Constructed by: LSWR
Year opened: 1860
Services: Passenger, freight
Types of traction: Loco-hauled
Electrified: No

Notes: Salisbury-Wilton – 2 track.
Wilton-Templecombe – single (passing place Gillingham).
Templecombe-Sherborne – 2 track.

The main route continues to the west as a double track section as far as Wilton Junction where the double track line to Westbury diverges to the right. The SR 'main line' to the west continuing as a single line to Templecombe, with a passing place at Gillingham. Double track then continues to the SR boundary at Sherborne. Frequency of traffic on this section is confined to two hourly passenger trains in each direction, with one or two ballast workings to and from quarries in the West of England. Class 50 No 50.050 departs from Gillingham on 7 July 1984 with the 15.10 Waterloo-Exeter service. *Colin J. Marsden*

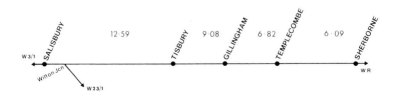

Route: W4
WATERLOO-READING

Section: W4/1 Clapham Junction-Barnes

Number of lines: 4
Signalling types: Colour light
Constructed by: LSWR
Year opened: 1846
Services: Passenger, freight
Types of traction: EMU,
Loco-hauled
Electrified: Yes

Diverging from the SWD main line at Clapham Junction is the quadruple tracked Windsor lines. This route continues for 3.16 miles to Barnes where the line becomes twin-tracked and carries on to Richmond and Hounslow. There are two intermediate stations between Clapham Junction and Barnes, at Wandsworth Town and Putney which are served by slow and semi-fast services. All stations have platform faces on all four lines, although those on the down fast at Wandsworth Town are out of use. 0.36 miles on the country side of Wandsworth Town is Point Pleasant Junction, where the line to East Putney and Wimbledon diverges. The Clapham-Putney section sees an abundance of passenger services all formed of EMU stock; an amount of freight traffic also traverses the tracks, mainly in the shape of inter-regional services arriving on the SR at Kew. 4EPB No 5121 approaches Putney on 27 October 1982 with the 10.16 Waterloo-Waterloo via Kingston service, a duty now performed by Class 455 stock. *Colin J. Marsden*

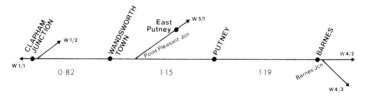

WANDSWORTH TOWN-EAST PUTNEY 1·00

24

Route: W4
WATERLOO-READING

Section: W4/ 2 Barnes-Feltham (via Twickenham)

Number of lines: 2
Signalling type: Colour light
Constructed by: LSWR
Year opened:
1846 (to Richmond),
1849 (to Feltham)
Services: Passenger, freight
Types of traction: EMU,
Loco-hauled
Electrified: Yes

After Barnes Junction, immediately at the country end of the station, the route to Feltham and then Ascot and Reading continues as a twin tracked section, with an additional 'up' running line between Twickenham and St Margarets. The LRT and LMR North London line connects by a reverse shunt at Richmond (tracks operated and maintained by the SR as far as Gunnersbury). At the country end of Twickenham the Strawberry Hill line diverges to the left. 0.50 miles after Whitton there is a connection with the Hounslow loop line, which also connects, in a down direction, with the main lines a further 0.40-miles south at Feltham Junction. Stations at Mortlake, Richmond, Whitton and Feltham have side platforms, whereas North Sheen has one island with platform faces on both sides. St Margarets has an island platform on the up and a side platform on the down, and Twickenham has two island platforms and two London facing bays. Passenger services over this route are usually formed of EMU stock, and a number of freight services also traverse lines in this section. A Class 455 stands at Twickenham with a Waterloo via Hounslow service.   *Colin J. Marsden*

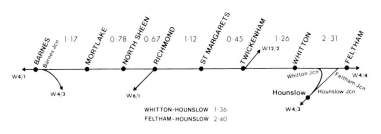

WHITTON-HOUNSLOW 1·36
FELTHAM-HOUNSLOW 2·40

Route: W4
WATERLOO-READING

Section: W4/3 Barnes-Feltham Junction/Whitton Junction (via Hounslow)

Number of lines: 2
Signalling type: Colour light
Constructed by: LSWR
Year opened: 1850
Services: Passenger, freight
Types of traction: EMU,
Loco-hauled
Electrified: Yes

Leaving the 'main' Reading route at Barnes and forming a loop, rejoining the 'main' at Feltham/Whitton Junction, is the Hounslow loop line, this being a twin tracked section served by suburban trains every 30 minutes. Diverging from this route near Kew Bridge station is the connection with the LMR at Kew East Junction. All stations on this route are of the side type. An amount of freight traffic uses this route, particularly to the south of Kew Bridge. Class 414 (2HAP) No 6002 departs from Chiswick with an 'up' service during 1983. Most passenger services are now in the hands of Class 455 stock.
Colin J. Marsden

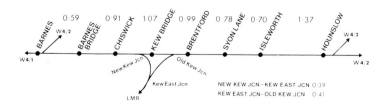

Route: W4
WATERLOO-READING

Section: W4/4 Feltham-Ascot

Number of lines: 2
Signalling type: Colour light
Constructed by: LSWR
Year opened: 1856

Services: Passenger, freight
Types of traction: EMU, Loco-hauled
Electrified: Yes

After the main Reading route departs from Feltham the twin tracks continue through Ashford and on to Staines where, at the London end, a small EMU servicing depot is situated. At the country end of the station the line to Windsor bears to the right and the Reading line veers to the left. The next notable point on the route is Virginia Water where the twin tracked route to Chertsey diverges to the left in the station. The line then continues through Longcross and Sunningdale to Ascot. Again all stations have side platforms. Passenger services are all formed of EMU stock and freight traffic is usually confined to the Feltham-Virginia Water section. 4VEP No 7753 slowly departs from Staines on 28 April 1984 with the 10.32 Reading-Waterloo service.
Colin J. Marsden

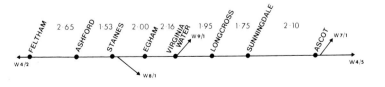

27

Route: W4
WATERLOO-READING

Section: W4/5 Ascot-Reading

Number of lines: 2
Signalling type: Colour light
Constructed by: LSWR (to Wokingham),
SER (Wokingham-Reading)
Year opened:
1856 (to Wokingham),
1849 (Wokingham-Reading)

Services: Passenger
Types of traction: EMU, DMU, Loco-hauled
Electrified: Yes
Notes: Occasional freight/departmental traffic

Directly at the country end of Ascot station the route to Camberley veers
sharp left, while the main line to Reading continues on as a double track
section through Bracknell and on to Wokingham, where at the London end of
the station the non-electrified route from Guildford joins in. The twin route
continues on to Reading where the SR line terminates in two bay platforms at
the London end of the WR station. 0.90-miles before the station is Reading
spur junction where a connection to the WR is provided. Trains on the section
between Ascot and Wokingham are usually of EMU stock but forward from
Wokingham they are supplemented by frequent DMUs emulating from
Gatwick/Tonbridge; Freight traffic traverses the route only infrequently. 2EPB
No 5772 leads an eight-car formation into Winnersh during the summer of
1984 with a Reading-Waterloo service. *Colin J. Marsden*

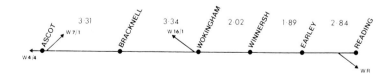

Route: W5
POINT PLEASANT JUNCTION-WIMBLEDON

Section: W5/1 Point Pleasant Junction-Wimbledon

Number of lines: 2
Signalling type: Colour light
Constructed by: LSWR
Year opened: 1889
Services: Empty Stock*
Types of traction: EMU, Loco-hauled
Electrified: Yes
Notes: *Line between East Putney-Wimbledon used jointly by BR/LRT, LRT

providing passenger service and BR using line for access to Wimbledon Park depot, through freight services and diversions.

The 3.75 miles from Wimbledon to a point just short of Putney Bridge station is operated by BR but the passenger service over the route is provided by LRT. However, BR do use the tracks from East Putney (where a connection with the Windsor lines exist) to Wimbledon Park for access into/out of East Wimbledon EMU Depot. The line is also used for occasional freight traffic. At Wimbledon the line feeds a four platform station adjacent to the main line station, each platform being capable of taking an eight-car train. From Wimbledon the route is a double tracked layout and the first station is Wimbledon Park which has a centre island platform. The next station is Southfields, also with an island platform followed by East Putney station with side platforms and additional faces on the disused BR side. A train of LRT 'D' stock stands at Wimbledon in 1981. *Colin J. Marsden*

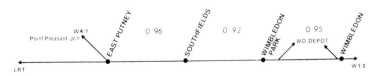

POINT PLEASANT JUNCTION-EAST PUTNEY 0.39

Route: W6
RICHMOND-GUNNERSBURY

Section: W6/1 Richmond-Gunnersbury

Number of lines: 2
Signalling type: Colour light
Constructed by: LSWR
Year opened: 1869
Services: Note 1
Types of traction: EMU (BR) and LRT
Electrified: Yes

Notes: Line managed by SR and used jointly with LRT District Line services.

The twin tracked route between Richmond and the London side of Gunnersbury is also managed by the SR although the passenger service is provided by the LMR North London line and the LRT District line. There are four platforms at Richmond which feed into one up and one down line shortly after the station; Kew Gardens being the first station on the line served by all trains and has side platforms. Gunnersbury provides an island platform and the junction between the LRT/LMR lines is at the London end of the station. A train of LRT 'D' stock departs from Richmond in 1982 forming a service to Upminster. *Colin J. Marsden*

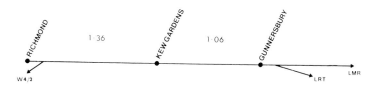

30

ASCOT-ASH VALE

Section: **W7/1 Ascot-Ash Vale**

Number of lines: Note 1
Signalling type: Colour light
Constructed by: LSWR
Year opened: 1878
Services: Passenger

Types of traction: EMU
Electrified: Yes
Notes: Ascot-Frimley – 2 track.
Frimley-Ash Vale single.

Diverging from the 'main' Reading line at Ascot and connecting into the Brookwood-Alton route at Ash Vale, is the 10.83 mile route known to staff as 'the branch'. The line has three intermediate stations, all having side platforms. Services are usually confined to a shuttle EMU passenger service from Guildford to Ascot; a few rush-hour trains operating to and from London. Between Frimley and Ash Vale the line is single track, controlled by the Tokenless block system. 4EPB No 5112 stands at Camberley while en route to Ascot. Today this route is usually worked by 4VEP or 4CIG units.
Colin J. Marsden

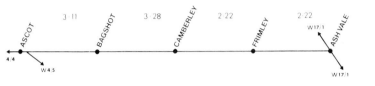

Route: W8
STAINES-WINDSOR

Section: W8/1 Staines-Windsor

Number of lines: 2

Signalling type: Colour light

Constructed by: LSWR

Year opened: 1849

Services: Passenger

Types of Traction: EMU

Electrified: Yes

Bearing off from the Reading route at the country end of Staines station is the 6.57 mile branch to Windsor & Eton Riverside which is served by a 30 minute interval service. The line is of double track layout and Windsor station has three platforms. The intermediate stations at Wraysbury and Datchet have side platforms, whilst that at Sunnymeads has an island. A short distance after Staines a left spur leads into Staines Oil Terminal, which was once the terminal of the GWR line to Staines from West Drayton. During summer months Windsor receives a few locomotive operated excursions, bringing a welcome change to the usual endless procession of EMUs. Class 455 No 581 arrives at Staines from the Windsor branch during the summer of 1984.
Colin J. Marsden

STAINES · W4/4 · 2·47 · WRAYSBURY · 1·10 · SUNNYMEADS · 1·19 · DATCHET · 1·81 · WINDSOR & ETON RIVERSIDE

W4/4

★ TO STAINES WEST OIL TERMINAL

Route: W9
VIRGINIA WATER-WEYBRIDGE/ BYFLEET JUNCTION

Section: W9/1 Virginia Water-Weybridge/ Byfleet Junction

Number of lines: 2
Signalling type: Colour light
Constructed by: LSWR
Year opened: 1848
Services: Passenger, freight
Types of traction: EMU, Loco-hauled
Electrified: Yes
Notes: Spur between Addlestone Junction-Byfleet Junction usually used by freight, empty stock and special services only.

A spur from the Reading route at Virginia Water is the short branch of 5.66 miles to Weybridge, which is served by a frequent shuttle from Staines. This route has two intermediate stations at Chertsey and Addlestone, both of which have side platforms. 0.96 miles on the Weybridge side of Addlestone lays Addlestone Junction where the freight only spur to Byfleet Junction diverges. Apart from the regular passenger services on the branch line a sizeable amount of freight traffic also uses the line. Class 455 No 5839 departs from Weybridge with a shuttle to Staines on 20 April 1984. The SWD main line can be seen in the background. *Colin J. Marsden*

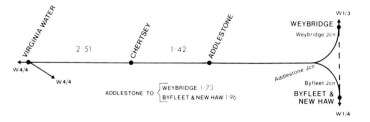

VIRGINIA WATER — CHERTSEY 2·51 — 1·42 — ADDLESTONE

W 4/4
W 4/4

ADDLESTONE TO { WEYBRIDGE 1·73 / BYFLEET & NEW HAW 1·96

W 1/3
WEYBRIDGE
Weybridge Jcn

Addlestone Jcn
Byfleet Jcn
BYFLEET & NEW HAW
W 1/4

Route: W10
RAYNES PARK-EPSOM

Section: W10/1 Raynes Park-Epsom

Number of lines: 2
Signalling type: Colour light
Constructed by: LSWR
Year opened: 1859

Services: Passenger, freight
Types of traction: EMU,
Loco-hauled
Electrified: Yes

Leaving the SWD main line at Raynes Park is the branch to Epsom and the
Central Division. This route is of twin tracked layout and is afforded a basic 3(
minute interval passenger service, however between Raynes Park and
Motspur Park this is supplemented by the Chessington line service. Motspur
Park station is of the island type and the junction for the Chessington line is
0.42 miles on the country side. The intermediate stations at Worcester Park
and Ewell West have side platforms, whilst facilities at Stoneleigh are on an
island. Directly at the London end of Epsom station is the junction with the
Sutton line. Class 455 No 5816 passes Raynes Park goods ground frame
signalbox on 14 June 1983 with an up service. *Colin J. Marsden*

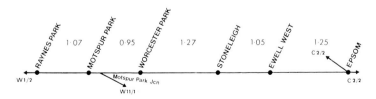

Route: W11
MOTSPUR PARK-CHESSINGTON

Section: W11/1 Motspur Park-Chessington

Number of lines: 2
Signalling type: Colour light
Constructed by: SR
Year opened: 1939
Services: Passenger, freight
Types of traction: EMU,
Loco-hauled
Electrified: Yes

The comparatively modern 1930s-built Chessington branch commences at Motspur Park Junction, a spur off the Raynes Park-Epsom line. This 3.78-mile branch serving four stations has double tracks with side platforms. Passenger services are provided by a 30 minute interval EMU service to and from Waterloo. Adjacent to Tolworth station and at the country end of Chessington South, are small coal sidings which are served by daily coal trains. Pulling out of Tolworth and heading for Malden Manor two Class 455s led by unit No 5820 are photographed on 12 March 1984. *Colin J. Marsden*

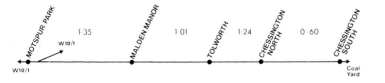

Route: W12
NEW MALDEN-TWICKENHAM/ SHEPPERTON

Section: W12/1 New Malden-Twickenham

Number of lines: 2
Signalling type: Colour light
Constructed by: LSWR
Year opened:
1869 to Kingston,
1863 to Twickenham
Services: Passenger
Types of traction: EMU
Electrified: Yes

Notes: EMU stabling and CM&EE testing section have small premises in triangle of line between Shacklegate Junction, Fulwell Junction and Strawberry Hill.

Another inner suburban branch is the Kingston line which diverges from the SWD main line at New Malden and running the 6.35 miles to Twickenham on the Waterloo-Windsor/Reading line. This route has a double track layout and all the five intermediate stations have side platforms. Kingston has an additional bay platform. Between Teddington and Strawberry Hill lays Shacklegate Junction where the branch to Shepperton bears off. At the Teddington end of Strawberry Hill station the line from Fulwell joins in, forming the third face of a triangle surrounding Strawberry Hill EMU and Research Depot. A Class 455 traverses between Hampton Wick and Teddington with a Waterloo-Shepperton service early in 1984
Colin J. Marsden

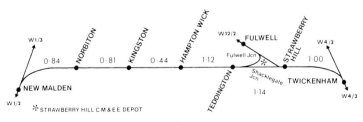

TEDDINGTON-FULWELL......1·22
FULWELL-STRAWBERRY HILL 0·66

Route: W12
NEW MALDEN-TWICKENHAM/
SHEPPERTON

Section: W12/2 Shacklegate Junction/
Strawberry Hill-Shepperton

Number of lines: 2
Signalling type: Colour light
Constructed by: LSWR
Year opened: 1864
Services: Passenger
Types of traction: EMU
Electrified: Yes

The 6.22-mile branch from Strawberry Hill/Shacklegate Junction to Shepperton has a double track layout, which also has the usual 30 minute service. There are five stations on this route, plus Kempton Park which is only open on race days. All have side platforms but Shepperton has only one with a small siding taking the position of the other. In addition to regular passenger services the branch sees frequent test trains involving new or refurbished stock operating to and from Strawberry Hill depot. Approaching Hampton Class 508 No 508.023 forms a down service. All Class 508s have now been re-allocated away from the SR to the Liverpool Division of the LMR. *Colin J. Marsden*

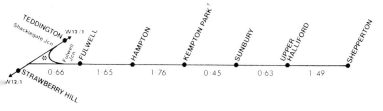

TEDDINGTON – FULWELL 1.22m
✳STRAWBERRY HILL C M & E E DEPOT
† OPEN ONLY ON SELECTED RACE DAYS

37

Route: W13
SURBITON-HAMPTON COURT

Section: W13/1 Surbiton-Hampton Court

Number of lines: 2
Signalling type: Colour light
Constructed by: LSWR
Year opened: 1849

Services: Passenger
Types of traction: EMU
Electrified: Yes

1.30 miles on the country side of Surbiton lays Hampton Court Junction where the short 2.60-mile branch to Hampton Court leaves the main line; however the actual branch commences (in a down direction) 0.25-miles after Surbiton station and runs parallel with the main line to Hampton Court Junction. The route has twin tracks with one intermediate station at Thames Ditton. Hampton Court station has two platforms with a siding occupying the position of the former third platform. The line receives a 30 minute interval service usually formed of Class 455 stock. On a snowy 10 January 1982 Class 508 No 508.020 stands at Hampton Court with the 11.14 service to Waterloo. *Colin J. Marsden*

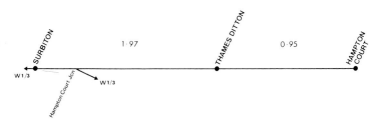

Route: **W14**
SURBITON-GUILDFORD
(via EFFINGHAM)

Section: W14/1 Surbiton-Effingham

Number of lines: 2
Signalling type: Colour light
Constructed by: LSWR
Year opened: 1885

Services: Passenger
Types of traction: EMU
Electrified: Yes

Also branching off from the SWD main line at Hampton Court Junction is the 6.54-mile 'New Line' to Guildford via Effingham. This route is of the twin track type and the section under discussion here as far as Effingham Junction has four intermediate stations, all except Hinchley Wood having side platforms; Hinchley Wood has an island platform. At the London end of Effingham Junction station is the converging junction with the Bookham and Epsom line. A half-hourly service operates on the 'New Line' and trains are usually formed of Class 455 stock, however a few peak period trains are formed of 4VEP or 4CIG stock. 4VEP No 7851 departs from Oxshott during 1984 with an up service.   *Colin J. Marsden*

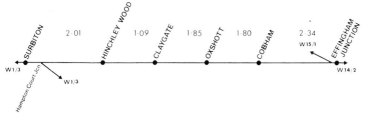

Route: W14
SURBITON-GUILDFORD
(via EFFINGHAM)

Section: W14/2 Effingham-Guildford

Number of lines: 2
Signalling type: Colour light
Constructed by: LSWR
Year opened: 1885

Services: Passenger
Types of traction: EMU
Electrified: Yes

At the country end of Effingham Junction is a small EMU stabling depot, which has regular movements in the shape of hourly terminating trains from Waterloo via Epsom. The main route continues as a twin track line on to Guildford, the three intermediate stations all having side platform facilities. At Guildford the line terminates in an eight-car bay platform but a connection is provided enabling trains to traverse to the through platforms. Class 455 No 5862 departs from Effingham Junction and passes the EMU depot where another of the class waits to form a service to Waterloo via Epsom.
Colin J. Marsden

EFFINGHAM JUNCTION — 1·02 — HORSLEY — 3·18 — CLANDON — 3·01 — LONDON ROAD — 1·54 — GUILDFORD

W14/1   W2/1

40

Route: W15
EFFINGHAM JUNCTION-
LEATHERHEAD

Section: W15/1 Effingham Junction-Leatherhead

Number of lines: 2
Signalling type: Colour light
Constructed by: LSWR
Year opened: 1885
Services: Passenger
Types of traction: EMU
Electrified: Yes

Connecting the Epsom-Dorking line with the New Guildford line between Leatherhead and Effingham Junction is a short branch of 4.23 miles with one intermediate station at Bookham. This section is of double track layout and Bookham station has side platforms. The passenger service consists of an hourly train between Waterloo and Effingham Junction which is usually operated by Class 455 units. Set No 5826 approaches Bookham station in this view with a down service. *Colin J. Marsden*

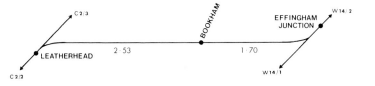

Route: W16/1
GUILDFORD-WOKINGHAM

Section: W16/1 Guildford-Wokingham

Number of lines: 2
Signalling type: Colour light
Constructed by: SER
Year opened: 1849
Services: Passenger, freight
Types of traction: EMU, DMU, Loco-hauled
Electrified: See Notes
Notes: Electrified Guildford-Ash Junction.

This section of line between Guildford and Wokingham, a distance of 18.9 miles is unusual in being electrified at both ends but not between Ash and Wokingham Junction. After leaving Guildford in a London direction the route climbs and veers left heading for Wanborough and Ash, both stations having side platforms. 0.79 miles onward from Ash is Aldershot South Junction where the connection with the Brookwood-Alton line bears off, taking the electric rail with it. The twin track now continues to Wokingham Junction as a non-electrified line, from where it is electrified into Wokingham station, as part of the Waterloo-Reading line. Services over the Guildford-Ash section consist of a half-hourly shuttle from Guildford to Ascot, and one slow and one fast DMU each hour between Reading-Gatwick/Tonbridge. Only a small amount of freight traffic traverses the route mainly to oil sidings at North Camp; a few inter-regional passenger services are also routed via the line. A WR three-car Class 119 DMU stands at Wokingham in 1982.
Colin J. Marsden

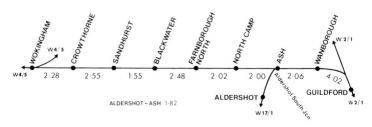

Route: **W17**
BROOKWOOD-ALTON

Section: W17/1 Brookwood-Alton

Number of lines: 2
Signalling type: Colour light
Constructed by: LSWR
Year opened:
1870 to Farnham,
1852 to Alton
Services:
Passenger, freight
Types of traction:
EMU,
Loco-hauled
Electrified: Yes

Diverging from the SWD main line at Pirbright Junction 1.5 miles the country side of Brookwood, is the Alton line. After Pirbright Junction the line heads for Ash Vale and just prior to the station the route from Ascot converges from the right. The next landmark is Aldershot North Junction where the connection from Aldershot South Junction and Ash converge. After a further 1.5 miles Aldershot station is reached which has an additional down 'loop' line served by an island platform; a side platform is provided on the 'up' side. The twin tracked route then continues to Farnham where, at the country end of the station, a small EMU depot is situated, plus a Civil Engineers' spoil tip. The main route continues on to Bentley and Alton. When this book went to press the line between Farnham and Alton had been singled.
Frequency of services on the Alton line is at 30 minute intervals as far as Farnham and hourly to Alton. Trains are usually formed of 4VEP stock. 4VEP No 7704 approaches Farnham in this view. Frequent ballast trains operate between Woking and Farnham.
Colin J. Marsden

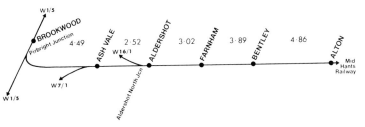

Route: W18
BASINGSTOKE-READING

Section: W18/1 Basingstoke-Reading

Number of lines: 2
Signalling type: Colour light
Constructed by: GWR
Year opened: 1848

Services: Passenger, freight
Types of traction: DMU, Loco-hauled
Electrified: No

Connecting the Southern and Western Regions between Basingstoke and Reading is a very useful link which sees considerable freight and passenger activity. The route, which is SR property only as far as Southcote Junction, is of twin track and has two intermediate stations, served only by local services. The line is not electrified and local weekday services are formed of SR DEMU stock, whilst on Sundays 4TC and Class 33/1 formations are used. A number of inter-regional services from Bournemouth, Poole and Weymouth to the Midlands use the route as does a large amount of freight traffic. On 25 April 1984 Class 47 No 47.533 takes the Reading line at Basingstoke with the 12.40 Poole-Manchester.   *Colin J. Marsden*

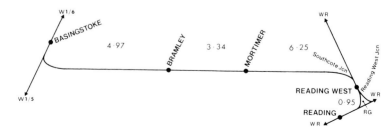

Route: W19
EASTLEIGH-FAREHAM

Section: W19/1 Eastleigh-Fareham

Number of lines: Note 1
Signalling type: Colour light
Year opened: 1842
Services: Passenger, freight
Types of traction: DMU,
Loco-hauled
Electrified: No

Notes: Eastleigh-Botley – 2
track.
Botley-Fareham – single.

Veering to the left directly after Eastleigh station is a 10.83-mile connection to
Fareham via Botley. The route from Eastleigh as far as Botley is of double
track but from a point just country end of Botley station the line to Fareham is
single track, operated by the Tokenless block system. At the Eastleigh end of
the line the route passes the side of Eastleigh Works and there is a right hand
junction taking stock/locomotives into Eastleigh depot. At the London side of
Botley a small Foster Yeoman stone terminal exists which receives at least
one train per day from the Westbury area, usually headed by two Class 37s or
a Class 56 locomotive. This route is not electrified and is usually worked by
three-car DEMU stock. *Michael J. Collins*

Route: W20
ST DENYS-HILSEA/FARLINGTON JUNCTION

Section: W20/1 St Denys-Fareham

Number of lines: 2
Signalling type: Colour light
Constructed by: LSWR
Year opened:
1866 St Denys-Netley,
1889 Netley-Fareham

Services: Passenger, freight
Types of traction: DMU,
Loco-hauled
Electrified: No

Another useful cross-country connection joins the Bournemouth main line with the Portsmouth line between St Denys and a point near Hilsea. At St Denys the branch connects with the main in the station area, the double tracked non-electried route continuing to Fareham, serving seven intermediate stations. Diverging from the route at Hamble is a short siding into Hamble BP oil terminal. Shortly before Fareham station the single line connection from Botley and Eastleigh converges. Services over this route are local DEMU trains between Portsmouth-Southampton-Salisbury and Reading, plus the approximately hourly Portsmouth-Westbury-Bristol/Cardiff services. 3H No 1125 stands at Bursledon with a train bound for Portsmouth.
Colin J. Marsden

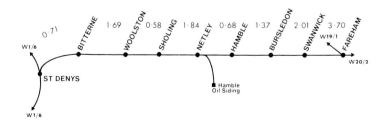

Route: W20
ST DENYS-HILSEA/FARLINGTON JUNCTION

Section: W20/2 Fareham-Hilsea/Farlington Junction

Number of lines: 2
Signalling type: Colour light
Constructed by: LSWR
Year opened: 1848

Services: Passenger, freight
Types of traction: DMU, Loco-hauled
Electrified: No

At the Portsmouth end of Fareham station is the junction with the 3.24-mile Bedenham Ministry of Defence siding which has very infrequent traffic. The main non-electrified twin track continues through Porchester and Cosham Junction where a junction either takes trains to Hilsea and on to Portsmouth, or to Bedhampton and thence Havant. Services over this route are either operated by DEMUs or Class 33s on trains of five or six Mk 1s operating the 'Wessex Rail' services. Slowing for the stop at Portchester 3H No 1128 works the 15.35 Reading-Portsmouth on 12 June 1982. *Colin J. Marsden*

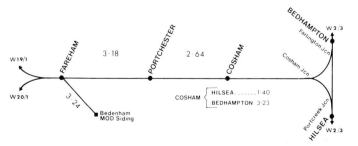

47

Route: W21
REDBRIDGE-SALISBURY

Section: W21/1 Redbridge-Salisbury

Number of lines: 2
Signalling type: Colour light
Constructed by: LSWR
Year opened:
1865 Redbridge-Romsey,
1847 Romsey-Salisbury
(Milford),
1859 Salisbury

(Milford-Tunnel Junction)
Services: Passenger, freight
Types of traction: DMU,
Loco-hauled
Electrified: No

Bearing right from the main Waterloo-Bournemouth line at the country end of Redbridge station is the branch to Salisbury, a non-electrified twin tracked route. After leaving the main line the branch travels through the Hampshire countryside for 5.42 miles before reaching Romsey where, prior to the station, the line from Eastleigh joins. After Romsey the line continues through Dunbridge and Dean before reaching Laverstock South Junction where trains can join the Basingstoke-Salisbury line in either direction. Trains traversing this route are mainly locomotive-hauled Portsmouth-Bristol/Cardiff services, with DEMUs providing a local stopping service. There is also considerable freight traffic which usually takes the direct Eastleigh line from Romsey. A '3H' DEMU passes Dean Hill sidings during the summer of 1982.
Colin J. Marsden

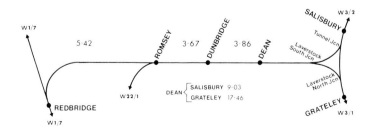

Route: W22
ROMSEY-EASTLEIGH

Section: W22/1 Romsey-Eastleigh

Number of lines: Single
Signalling type: Colour light
Constructed by: LSWR
Year opened: 1847
Services: Freight*
Type of traction:
Loco-hauled
Electrified: No

Notes: *Passed for passenger train operation.

The 7.25-mile connection between Romsey and Eastleigh is essentially a freight only route but is passed for passenger train operation if required. Freight services are mainly from the WR to Eastleigh. This is a single line route operated by the Tokenless Block system. Class 33 No 33.004 pulls off the Romsey line at Eastleigh with a stone train bound for the Central Division during the summer of 1984. *Colin J. Marsden*

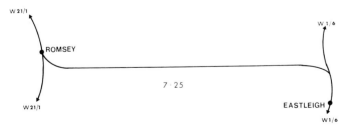

W 21/1

ROMSEY

W 21/1

7·25

W 1/6

EASTLEIGH

W 1/6

Route: W23
SALISBURY-WARMINSTER

Section: W23/1 Salisbury-Warminster

Number of lines: 2
Signalling type: Colour light
Constructed by: GWR
Year opened: 1856
Services: Passenger, freight
Type of traction:
Loco-hauled
Electrified: No

Veering right from the Salisbury-West of England main line at Wilton
Junction 1.80 miles after Salisbury is the twin tracked route to Westbury
which is under SR control to Heytesbury, a closed station on the Salisbury
side of Warminster. This line has no intermediate stations and is used by the
Portsmouth-Bristol/Cardiff services punctuated by frequent stone trains en
route to and from the Somerset quarries. Class 56 No 56.033 enters SR
territory at Heytesbury on 31 August 1984 with a stone working to Botley.
Colin J. Marsden

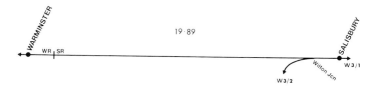

Route: W24
BROCKENHURST-LYMINGTON PIER

Section: W24/1 Brockenhurst-Lymington Pier

Number of lines: Single
Signalling type: Colour light
Constructed by: LSWR
Year opened: 1858
Services: Passenger
Type of traction: EMU
Electrified: Yes

To convey passengers to Lymington Pier, where a ferry service is provided to the Isle of Wight, a short 5.36-mile branch runs from Brockenhurst, with an intermediate passenger station at Lymington Town. A small staff halt is also situated 0.94 miles on the Brockenhurst side of Lymington Town. After leaving Brockenhurst this branch runs parallel with the main line to Lymington Junction where it sweeps to the left. Services on this single line are confined to a shuttle to and from Brockenhurst, usually formed of Class 414 (HAP) or Class 423 (VEP) stock. 2HAP No 6105 approaches Lymington Junction in 1982 bound for Brockenhurst. *Colin J. Marsden*

Route: W25
RYDE PIER HEAD-SHANKLIN

Section: W25/1 Ryde Pier Head-Shanklin

Number of lines: 2*
Signalling type: Colour light, semaphore
Constructed by:
LBSCR/LSWR Joint
Isle of Wight Railway

Year opened: 1864
Services: Passenger
Types of traction: EMU
Electrified: Yes
Notes: *Single: Smallbrook Junction-Brading.

The unique 8.36-mile line on the Isle of Wight from Ryde Pier Head to Shanklin, although having no physical connection with the SR, is managed and staffed by BR Southern. The present route, which is only a fraction of the original island railway system, was opened in its present form from March 1967. The line is basically double tracked except between Smallbrook Junction and Brading which is single, it has four intermediate stops and is worked by former London Transport tube size stock. The only divergence from the route is at Ryde St Johns Road where a depot and small workshop is situated. 4VEC No 485.043 approaches Sandown with the 10.37 Ryde-Shanklin on 14 June 1982. *Colin J. Marsden*

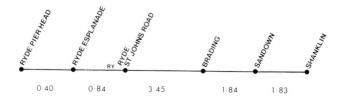

Route: W26
WATERLOO-BANK

Section: W26/1 Waterloo-Bank

Number of lines: 2
Signalling type: Colour light
Constructed by: LSWR
Year opened: 1898
Services: Passenger
Type of traction: EMU (Tube size)
Electrified: Yes

Another route independent of the main line but controlled by the SR is the 1.39-mile Waterloo & City railway, connecting Waterloo with the Bank in the City of London. This route runs through two single bore tunnels and is operated by purpose built tube size stock, working on week days and Saturday mornings only. The station at Bank has one island platform whilst Waterloo has two side platforms. A yard, depot and small workshop facilities exist at the Waterloo end of the line. Shortly after Waterloo station there is a reverse shunt giving access into the 'hydraulic lift' which provides a connection with the main line above. Car No S56 stands at Waterloo on 8 October 1980. Trains are either formed of two motor coaches coupled together, or two motor coaches with three trailers between. *Colin J. Marsden*

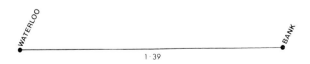

WATERLOO   1·39   BANK

Route: C1
VICTORIA-BRIGHTON

Section: C1/1 Victoria-Clapham Junction

Number of lines: 4
Signalling type: Colour light
Constructed by: LBSCR
Year opened: 1858
Services: Passenger

Types of traction: EMU, DMU, Loco-hauled
Electrified: Yes
Notes: Occasional freight/departmental traffic.

The most complex of individual routes in this product is the Victoria-Clapham Junction section, including the lines to and via Stewarts Lane. The basic route map is shown below but a more detailed illustration is given opposite. The route from Victoria to Clapham Junction is basically of the four tracked type, with additional running lines in the close proximity to Victoria. The layout of tracks is such that (from Victoria) the local or slow tracks are on the left and the fast lines on the right. The section mainly sees passenger traffic predominantly formed of EMU stock but the 15 minute interval 'Gatwick Express' service hauled by Class 73s breaks this monopoly. The line between the LMR and Factory Junction via Culvert Road Junction sees a sizeable amount of freight train activity, often bringing foreign motive power to the SR. Facelifted 4EPB No 5408 stands at Clapham Junction on 19 August 1982 with a train from Epsom Downs to Victoria. *Colin J. Marsden*

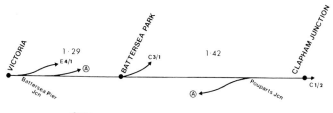

Ⓐ TO STEWARTS LANE &
FREIGHT LINE COMPLEX

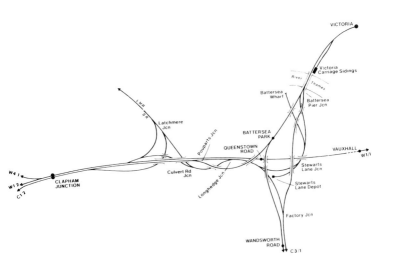

One of the major SR depots – Stewarts Lane – is situated within this section. Apart from being the home of all Class 73s and the Gatwick Express stock, the depot has large maintenance facilities for EMUs and fuelling equipment for diesel traction; the depot also houses the VSOE Pullman stock. Pulling slowly out of the carriage sidings and passing the former steam shed Class 33 No 33.056 *The Burma Star* hauls the VSOE Pullmans to Victoria on 9 May 1984. In the background is the flyover carrying the Battersea Park-Wandsworth Road Line. *Colin J. Marsden*

Route: C1
VICTORIA-BRIGHTON
Section: C1/2 Clapham Junction-Selhurst

Number of lines: 4
Signalling type: Colour light
Constructed by: LBSCR
Year opened:
1858 to Balham,

1862 to Selhurst
Services: Passenger, freight
Types of traction: EMU,
DMU, Loco-hauled
Electrified: Yes

The Central section of Clapham Junction has four main running lines with
platforms on each. In addition the twin tracked line to Latchmere Junction
also has platform facilities. After departing from Clapham Junction the
quadruple track passes through Wandsworth Common and Balham, both of
which have platform faces on all lines. Shortly after Balham station the twin
track route to Streatham leaves the main line which continues to Streatham
North Junction, where a facing connection is made with Streatham South
Junction and thence Tooting or Mitcham Junction. The main line then passes
under the Streatham-Mitcham line and a spur connection converges from
Streatham Junction at the London end of Streatham Common station. The
four track route then continues to Selhurst past Norbury and Thornton Heath.
4EPB No 5351 traverses the down local line near Wandsworth Common in
the summer of 1984 while forming a Victoria-Epsom Downs service.
Colin J. Marsden

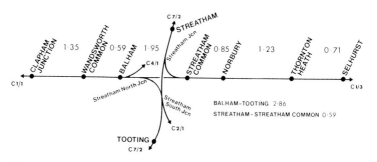

Route: C1
VICTORIA-BRIGHTON

Section: C1/3 Selhurst-Purley

Number of lines: 4
Signalling type: Colour light
Constructed by: LBSCR
Year opened: 1841

Services: Passenger, freight
Types of traction: EMU, DMU, Loco-hauled
Electrified: Yes

At the country end of Selhurst station a right spur leads into the large Selhurst EMU depot and forms a connection with Norwood Junction, while a right lead provides a junction with the West Croydon line. After a further short distance the line from Norwood Junction joins, and the now five track mainly reversable route progresses to East Croydon, where platform facilities exist on all lines. From East Croydon station a five track layout continues past South Croydon where platforms are again provided on all lines. After a further 0.48 mile the line to Sanderstead bears left and the four track route continues to Purley. Traffic over this section consists of suburban and main line services, the majority being formed of EMUs, however the frequent 'Gatwick Express' services provide a welcome break, as do the infrequent inter-regional services to and from the Midlands and freight traffic. Services to and from the Sanderstead line are formed of SR DEMU stock. 4EPB No 5021 departs from East Croydon and heads for Windmill Bridge Junction with a Caterham-London Bridge train. *Colin J. Marsden*

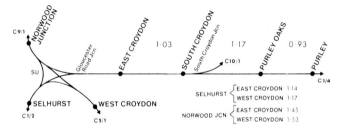

Route: C1
VICTORIA-BRIGHTON

Section: C1/4 Purley-Gatwick Airport
Number of lines: 4
Signalling type: Colour light
Constructed by: LBSCR
Year opened: 1841
Services:
Passenger, freight
Types of traction:
EMU,
Loco-hauled
Electrified: Yes

After Purley the next landmark reached is Coulsdon North Junction where the fast and slow tracks part company. The fast route takes the 'quarry line' to Earlswood with no intermediate stations, whilst the twin local tracks pass Coulsdon South and Merstham, both with side platforms, before reaching Redhill station which has two fast centre tracks and an up 'loop' line in addition to the normal up and down platform lines. At the country end of Redhill the non-electrified route to Tonbridge bears left and the line to Reigate and eventually Guildford to the right. The main route reverts back to two tracks and continues to Earlswood where, at the London end of the station, the 'quarry line' rejoins, and the route now of four tracks continues on through Salfords and Horley to Gatwick Airport. Traffic over this section, both on the 'Quarry' and Redhill lines is quite intense, main line services including the 'Gatwick Express' usually taking the Quarry route. A few inter-regional passenger trains also traverse the tracks as does a small amount of freight traffic. The cross-country line from Reading to Tonbridge, as well as the regular Reading-Gatwick service brings WR DMMU stock to this section. A 'Gatwick Express' service headed by Class 73 No 73.123 *Gatwick Express* approaches Horley during the summer of 1984 with a down service. *Colin J. Marsden*

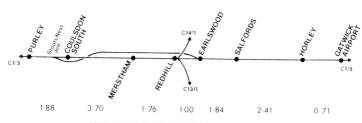

STOATS NEST JUNCTION-EARLSWOOD (Quarry Line) 6·67

Route: C1
VICTORIA-BRIGHTON

Section: C1/5 Gatwick Airport-Burgess Hill

Number of lines: 2
Signalling type: Colour light
Constructed by: LBSCR
Year opened: 1841
Services: Passenger, freight
Types of traction: EMU, Loco-hauled
Electrified: Yes

Onwards from Gatwick Airport the quadruple tracks continue to Three Bridges, passing several aggregate sidings on route. At the country end of Three Bridges station there is a parting of the ways, the Brighton line continuing straight with the twin tracked Horsham route diverging to the right. The now twinned Brighton line passes through Balcombe with its side platforms, before reaching Copyhold Junction, where the freight branch to Ardingly converges on the down side. The route continues through Haywards Heath to Wivelsfield, where at the country end of the station, the line to Lewes bears left the Brighton main traversing another 0.83 miles to Burgess Hill. Traffic over this stretch is mainly of the EMU type with infrequent locomotive-hauled passenger and freight services. 4CIG No 7437 heads south between Haywards Heath and Wivelsfield on 9 March 1982 with a Victoria-Brighton semi-fast service. *Colin J. Marsden*

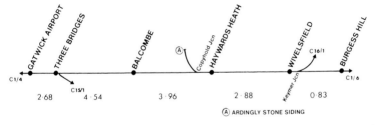

Ⓐ ARDINGLY STONE SIDING

Route: C1
VICTORIA-BRIGHTON

Section: C1/6 Burgess Hill-Brighton

Number of lines: 2
Signalling type: Colour light
Constructed by: LBSCR
Year opened: 1841

Services: Passenger, freight
Types of traction: EMU, Loco-hauled
Electrified: Yes

The main twin tracked route continues from Burgess Hill through Hassocks and on to Preston Park where, soon after the station, a right hand spur connects with the 'Coastway' line to Hove. Adjacent to Preston Park station are carriage sidings forming part of Brighton depot. As the route continues south into Brighton station additional running lines converge from the east and west 'Coastway' routes. Brighton locomotive stabling point is situated outside the station in the junction of the main and 'West Coastway' lines. The route between Burgess Hill and Brighton has frequent fast and stopping services from London, supplemented by some inter-regional services from the Midlands. Regular 'Coastway' services also operate to and from Brighton. A 12-car formation led by 4VEP No 7871 departs from Patcham Tunnel with a Littlehampton-Hove-Victoria train during 1982. *Colin J. Marsden*

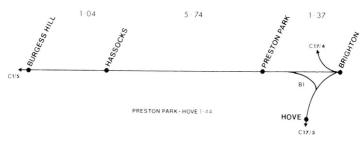

Route: C2
STREATHAM-ARUNDEL

Section: C2/1 Streatham-Sutton

Number of lines: 2
Signalling type: Colour light
Constructed by: LBSCR
Year opened: 1868

Services: Passenger
Type of traction: EMU
Electrified: Yes

Another quite complex route with a number of convergences and diversions is the Streatham-Sutton line. This is basically a twin tracked route with three intermediate stations, all having side platforms. Directly after Streatham station a left lead connects with the Central Division main line in a down direction, while shortly after a converging line from Streatham North Junction brings a connection into Streatham South Junction, where a facing connection also exists with the line to Tooting. The route then continues on to Mitcham Junction where, at the London end of the station, the Wimbledon line joins in. After the station the main route to Sutton bears right while the line to West Croydon carries on, passing through Hackbridge and Carshalton; Sutton Junction is then reached where the line from West Croydon connects. Facelifted 4EPB No 5431 approaches Mitcham Junction from the Sutton line in mid 1984. The signalbox on the left has now been abolished. *Colin J. Marsden*

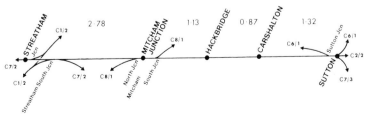

61

Route: C2
STREATHAM-ARUNDEL

Section: C2/2 Sutton-Leatherhead

Number of lines: 2
Signalling type: Colour light
Constructed by: LBSCR
Year opened: 1847 to Epsom,

1867 to Leatherhead
Services: Passenger
Type of traction: EMU
Electrified: Yes

After leaving Sutton two further routes diverge from the main line, first a left branch takes the single line to Epsom Downs, which is closely followed by a right branch heading for Wimbledon. The main now continues on through two intermediate stations before reaching Epsom where, at the London end of the station, the line from Raynes Park joins in. After departing from Epsom the double tracked route passes Ashtead before reaching Leatherhead. Stations on this route are of the side type except for Epsom which has two island platforms and four faces. Traffic is basically confined to 30 minute interval suburban services, however some Central Section Littlehampton trains are routed via this line, as are infrequent freight trains. The country side of Epsom also sees Western section trains operating between Waterloo-Effingham Junction/Dorking and Horsham. An 8CIG formation led by No 7436 is seen between Epsom and Ashtead during the summer of 1984 with a Victoria-Bognor Regis services. *Colin J. Marsden*

Route: C2
STREATHAM-ARUNDEL

Section: C2/3 Leatherhead-Horsham

Number of lines: 2
Signalling type: Colour light, semaphore
Constructed by: LBSCR
Year opened: 1867

Services: Passenger
Types of traction: EMU
Electrified: Yes
Notes: Occasional freight/departmental traffic.

At the country end of Leatherhead station the short cross-country connection to Effingham bears right, whilst the twin tracked route continues on through Boxhill with side platforms, to Dorking, which has an additional down loop line; platform facilities consisting of a side platform on the 'up' and an island on the 'down'. There is a small EMU stabling depot adjacent to the station. The route now continues over the Surrey/West Sussex border and on to Horsham through three intermediate stations, all with side platforms. As the line approaches Horsham the route from Three Bridges converges from the left. Horsham station has an additional 'up' and 'down' platform line providing two 12-car length island platforms. Just prior to Horsham station there is a sizeable yard on the right which houses the Chipmans weedkilling train and stock for the power supply section. 4EPB No 5452 approaches Dorking with a Horsham-Victoria train. *Colin J. Marsden*

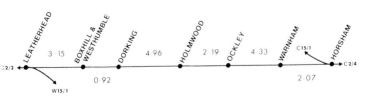

Route: C2
STREATHAM-ARUNDEL

Section: C2/4 Horsham-Arundel

Number of lines: 2
Signalling type: Colour light
Constructed by: LBSCR
Year opened:
1859 to Pulborough,

1863 to Arundel
Services: Passenger
Type of traction: EMU
Electrified: Yes

The 17.07-mile section from Horsham to Arundel is a twin tracked route with three intermediate stations at Christs Hospital, Billingshurst and Pulborough. No special features or junctions exist on this section and services are basically hourly between Bognor Regis and London, with a few additional 'off peak' slow trains between Littlehampton and Victoria. Several south coast commuter trains are routed via this line taking congestion away from the main Brighton line. Trains on this section are usually formed of EMU stock. Two 4VEP units led by No 7723 arrive at Horsham during the summer of 1982. *Colin J. Marsden*

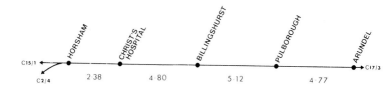

C15/1
C2/4
HORSHAM   CHRIST'S HOSPITAL   BILLINGSHURST   PULBOROUGH   ARUNDEL   C17/3
2·38   4·80   5·12   4·77

Route: C3
VICTORIA-LONDON BRIDGE

Section: C3/1 Victoria-London Bridge

Number of lines: 2
Signalling type: Colour light
Constructed by: LBSCR
Year opened: 1866
Services: Passenger
Type of traction: EMU
Electrified: Yes

The 8.63-mile twin tracked route linking Victoria and London Bridge is known as the 'South London Line' (SLL). It diverges from the CD main at Battersea Park and serves six intermediate stations with a large number of junctions diverting from it. Between Battersea Park and Peckham Rye SED tracks run parallel which have inter-connecting points at either end. The main inter-sections are: directly after crossing the Grosvenor Bridge outside Victoria the SED line to Kent bears left, as does a connection to Stewarts Lane and the non-passenger tracks to Culvert Road junction. Prior to Wandsworth Road station comes Factory Junction where there is another connection with the Stewarts Lane area freight lines. The next inter-sections are at Canterbury Road junction and Cambria junction where there is a link with the Holborn Viaduct line. The route then passes Denmark Hill before the line from Tulse Hill joins at Peckham Rye Junction just prior to Peckham Rye station. There is a junction between the SLL and the adjacent SED line near Peckham Rye where freight trains that have traversed the SLL from Factory Junction can be diverted to the SED tracks. The line continues through Queens Road (Peckham) and South Bermondsey before running parallel with the CD/SED main lines into London Bridge. The SLL only has peak hour trains but some stations are served by trains from other routes throughout the day. 2EPB No 5654 passes Denmark Hill with a South London Line train on 18 February 1975. *Brian Morrison*

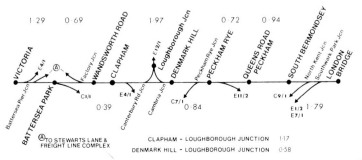

CLAPHAM – LOUGHBOROUGH JUNCTION   1·17
DENMARK HILL – LOUGHBOROUGH JUNCTION   0·58

Route: C4
BALHAM-BECKENHAM JUNCTION

Section: C4/1 Balham-Beckenham Junction

Number of lines: 2
Signalling type: Colour light
Constructed by:
LBSCR/SECR
Year opened: 1858
Services: Passenger, freight
Types of traction: EMU,
Loco-hauled
Electrified: Yes

The Central suburban route to Beckenham Junction diverges from the main
CD line at Balham Junction. Basically twin tracked it continues past
Streatham Hill carriage sidings to Streatham Hill station which has side
platforms and a four train per hour service to and from Victoria. After the
station the lines continue the 0.68 miles to Leigham Junction where a facing
connection provides access to Tulse Hill; a further 0.34 mile finds West
Norwood Junction where a converging connection is made from the Tulse
Hill line. Continuing through West Norwood and Gipsy Hill it reaches Crystal
Palace where a left spur in the station takes a connection to Sydenham
Junction and Sydenham. 0.83-miles after Crystal Palace is Bromley Junction
where a connection with the Annerley-Norwood Junction route is provided.
The Beckenham Junction line from this point and through Birkbeck is a single
line section operated by Tokenless block. Apart from regular suburban
passenger services usually operated by Class 455 and EPB stock the line also
sees an amount of freight traffic which traverses the route as far as Bromley
Junction where it bears right for Norwood Junction and the Brighton line.
4EPB No 5025 approaches Streatham Hill and is seen passing the carriage
sidings with a Victoria-Epsom Downs services. *Colin J. Marsden*

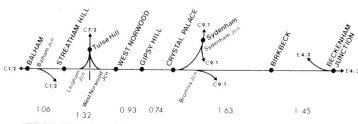

STREATHAM HILL-TULSE HILL 1·09
TULSE HILL-WEST NORWOOD 0·73

CRYSTAL PALACE - SYDENHAM 1·15

Route: C5
CRYSTAL PALACE-WEST CROYDON

Section: C5/1 Crystal Palace-West Croydon

Number of lines: 2
Signalling type: Colour light
Constructed by: LBSCR
Year opened:
1854 to Norwood,
1839 to West Croydon
Services: Passenger, freight
Types of traction: EMU,
loco-hauled
Electrified: Yes

The line connecting Crystal Palace with Norwood Junction and West Croydon is complicated to say the least, and apart from regular passenger services it provides an invaluable line for both freight traffic or passenger diversions away from the main line. The lines from Bromley Junction join onto the main London Bridge-East Croydon route at the London end of Norwood Junction station, being a four tracked route. After Norwood Junction station, where platform faces exist on all tracks, the main route continues through Norwood Junction to Windmill Bridge Junction and on to East Croydon. However a route to West Croydon passes over the East Croydon line and then under the Selhurst-East Croydon route before passing through Cottage Junction and on to West Croydon. Facelifted 4EPB No 5431 descends the steep connection with Bromley Junction at Norwood Junction in 1984 with a Victoria-West Croydon-Epsom Downs train. *Colin J. Marsden*

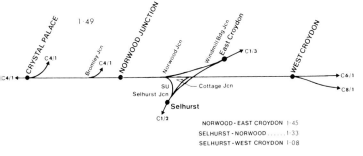

NORWOOD - EAST CROYDON 1·45
SELHURST - NORWOOD ......1·33
SELHURST - WEST CROYDON 1·08

Route: C6
WEST CROYDON-EPSOM DOWN

Section: C6/1 West Croydon-Epsom Downs

Number of lines: 2
Signalling type: Colour light
Constructed by: LBSCR
Year opened: 1847 to Sutton,
1865 to Epsom Downs
Services: Passenger
Type of traction: EMU
Electrified: Yes

The route to the country side of West Croydon consists of three tracks – the double tracked Sutton route and the single line to Wimbledon via Mitcham, which diverges sharp right after approximately 1-mile. The double track continues to Sutton via Waddon, Wallington and Carshalton Beeches; directly at the London end of Sutton station the Mitcham Junction route converges from the left. After leaving Sutton the lines to Wimbledon and Epsom continue on while our route to Epsom Downs, now a single track, bears left and passes through Belmont and Banstead towards the terminus. The West Croydon-Sutton route has three trains per hour in each direction, whilst the Epsom Downs branch has only an hourly service. A 4EPB arrives Banstead station with an 'up' service during 1984. *Colin J. Marsden*

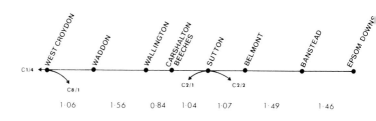

Route: C7
PECKHAM RYE-SUTTON
(via WIMBLEDON)

Section: C7/1 Peckham Rye-Tulse Hill

Number of lines: 2
Signalling type: Colour light
Constructed by: LBSCR
Year opened: 1868

Services: Passenger
Type of traction: EMU
Electrified: Yes

This short 2.64-mile connecting line joins the South London Line at Peckham Rye with Tulse Hill, serving intermediate stations at East Dulwich and North Dulwich. After Peckham Rye the route leaves the South London line at Peckham Rye Junction and continues as a double tracked route to the London end of Tulse Hill where the line from Herne Hill converges from the right. The station has four platform lines which are arranged with two side faces and one island. At the country end a three-way junction exists; the line to Streatham and thus Wimbledon or Mitcham continues as the straight route, whilst both a left and right divergence takes trains on to the Streatham Hill-West Norwood line. 4EPB No 5429 emerges from Knights Hill Tunnel and approaches Tulse Hill station with a service bound for Reigate.
Colin J. Marsden

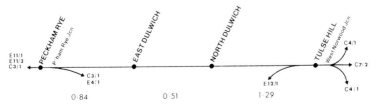

Route: C7
PECKHAM RYE-SUTTON
(via WIMBLEDON)

Section: C7/2 Tulse Hill-Wimbledon

Number of lines: 2
Signalling type: Colour light
Constructed by: LBSCR
(Joint LSWR
Streatham-Wimbledon)

Year opened: 1868
Services: Passenger
Type of traction: EMU
Electrified: Yes

After taking the straight or main route from Tulse Hill the line heads 1.29 miles to Streatham where at the country end of the station a facing connection is provided to the CD main line and Streatham Common. After a further short distance a right convergence at Streatham South Junction connects from Balham and Streatham North Junction. At the same point the route to Wimbledon bears sharp right and the straight route continues to Mitcham Junction. The Wimbledon line then passes through Tooting and Haydons Road, both of which have side platforms, before reaching Wimbledon, where there is a connection with the SWD. Services over this route are normally half-hourly and formed of Class 455 or EPB stock. A Wimbledon bound train arrives at Tulse Hill in the summer of 1984 lead by 2EPB No 5651. *Colin J. Marsden*

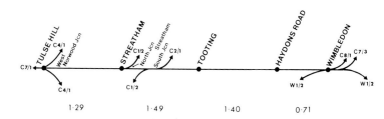

Route: C7
PECKHAM RYE-SUTTON
(via WIMBLEDON)

Section: C7/3 Wimbledon-Sutton

Number of lines: 2
Signalling type: Colour light
Constructed by: SR
Year opened: 1930

Services: Passenger
Type of traction: EMU
Electrified: Yes

Onwards from Wimbledon to Sutton the CD twin tracks continue to
Wimbledon West Junction, adjacent to the SWD main line, the track then
bears left and passes through six intermediate stations before reaching
Sutton in an 'up' direction joining the 'main' line at the south end of the
station. Stations on this route are a mixture of island and side types, all of
which can accommodate an eight-car train. Services operate at 30 minute
intervals and are usually formed of Class 455 or EPB stock. A six-car EPB
formation led by unit No 5446 approaches Wimbledon with an 'up' train.
Note the SWD tracks on the right.   *Colin J. Marsden*

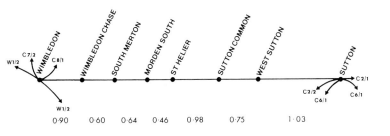

Route: C8
WIMBLEDON-WEST CROYDON

Section: C8/1 Wimbledon-West Croydon

Number of lines: Single*
Signalling type: Colour light
Constructed by: LBSCR
Year opened: 1885
Services: Passenger
Type of traction: EMU
Electrified: Yes
Notes: *Passing places at Mitcham Junction and Waddon Marsh.

One of the few 'inner suburban' routes that is predominantly single track is the Wimbledon-West Croydon via Mitcham Junction line. This 6.25-mile branch diverges left at the country end of Wimbledon station and is of double track to Merton Park, single track taking over from this point to the Croydon side of Mitcham where two tracks continue as far as Mitcham South Junction, from where single line operation continues to West Croydon, with a passing place at Waddon Marsh. At the London end of Mitcham Junction the line from Streatham joins in, and at the country end of the station diverges right for Sutton. Services over this route are two per hour in each direction and are usually formed of 2EPB stock. Unit No 6311 stops at Morden Road with a West Croydon bound train. *Colin J. Marsden*

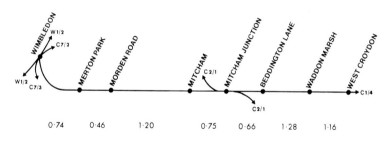

Route: C9
LONDON BRIDGE-NORWOOD JUNCTION

Section: C9/1 London Bridge (Central Section)-Norwood Junction

Number of lines: 4
Signalling type: Colour light
Constructed by: LBSCR
Year opened: 1839
Services: Passenger, freight
Types of traction: EMU, DMU, Loco-hauled
Electrified: Yes

Apart from Victoria the Central Division also operates a number of its main line and suburban services from London Bridge, where 50% of the station is devoted to CD services. The Central tracks travel adjacent to the SED as far as Southwark Park Junction where the CD quadruple tracks bear right and head for New Cross Gate, a station which is also served by LRT Metropolitan line services. The four track configuration continues via four intermediate stations to Sydenham Junction where a right divergence connects with Crystal Palace. The main line then progresses through Penge West and Annerly before reaching Bromley Junction where the Crystal Palace-Birkbeck line has a connection; the four tracks then go on to Norwood Junction. Traffic over this route is a mixture of main line and suburban EMU/DEMU services, which are punctuated by infrequent freight services. 4VEP No 7876 arrives at Forest Hill on the down local line with a London Bridge-Caterham service.
Colin J. Marsden

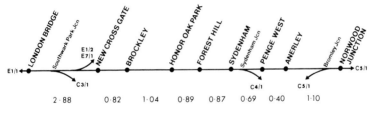

Route: C10
SOUTH CROYDON-
EAST GRINSTEAD/UCKFIELD

Section: C10/1 South Croydon-Hurst Green

Number of lines: 2
Signalling type: Semaphore, colour light
Constructed by: LBSCR

Year opened: 1884
Services: Passenger
Type of traction: DMU
Electrified: No

Branching left from the CD Brighton line at South Croydon Junction are the non-electrified routes to East Grinstead and Uckfield. The third rail is available as far as the first station on the line – Sanderstead. The route then continues through three intermediate stations before reaching Oxted where most services split, the front portion going to Uckfield and the rear to East Grinstead. This route then continues on to Hurst Green where, at the country end of the station, the lines to Uckfield and East Grinstead part company. The route is all of double track and stations have side platforms. Services are formed of DEMU stock, usually of the Class 205 or 207 type. Class 207 No 1301 arrives at Sanderstead on 26 January 1984 with an up train.
Brian Morrison

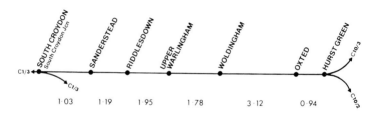

Route: **C10**
SOUTH CROYDON-
EAST GRINSTEAD/UCKFIELD

Section: C10/2 Hurst Green-East Grinstead

Number of lines: 2

Signalling type: Semaphore, Colour light

Constructed by: LBSCR

Year opened: 1884

Services: Passenger

Type of traction: DMU

Electrified: No

The 8.51-mile branch from Hurst Green to East Grinstead has two intermediate stations at Lingfield and Dormans, both of which have side platforms. It is basically an hourly service operated by DEMU stock, with some additional rush hour services. No branch lines diverge from this route. Class 207 No 1315 stands at Dormans in October 1984 with an up service.
Colin J. Marsden

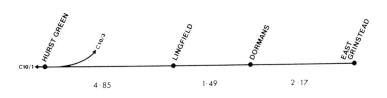

Route: C10
SOUTH CROYDON-
EAST GRINSTEAD/UCKFIELD

Section: C10/3 Hurst Green-Uckfield

Number of lines: 2

Signalling type: Colour light, semaphore

Constructed by: LBSCR

Year opened: 1868-88

Services: Passenger

Type of traction: DMU

Electrified: No

The Uckfield branch from Hurst Green has a total length of 23.89 miles and traverses through Surrey, Kent and East Sussex. After Hurst Green the double track configuration passes through four intermediate stations before reaching the first significant landmark – Birchden Junction, where the short branch from Tunbridge Wells joins in and terminates at the next station, Eridge, which has additional bay platforms. The main route then continues on to Uckfield as double track with two intermediate stations. This view shows Eridge station with an Uckfield-London service on the 'up' main line, and a '3D' unit forming the shuttle to Tunbridge Wells on the right in the bay platform. The branch between Tunbridge Wells and Eridge closed in July 1985. *Colin J. Marsden*

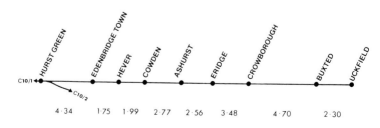

PURLEY-TATTENHAM CORNER

Section: C11/1 Purley-Tattenham Corner

Number of lines: 2
Signalling type: Colour light
Constructed by: SECR
Year opened: 1901

Services: Passenger
Type of traction: EMU
Electrified: Yes

The twin tracked suburban branch of 8.30 miles to Tattenham Corner diverges from the CD main line at Purley and soon after the divergence the line to Caterham bears left. There are no other branches or junctions on this route which is usually operated by EPB stock on a 30 minute interval basis. Each year this branch is in the news when HM The Queen travels to the Derby at Epsom Racecourse by train from Victoria to Tattenham Corner. Except for CCE traffic, this is the only time a locomotive visits the line. 2EPB No 5652 stops at Chipstead en route for Tattenham Corner. *Colin J. Marsden*

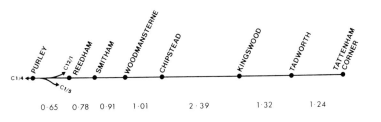

Route: C12
PURLEY-CATERHAM

Section: C12/1 Purley-Caterham

Number of lines: 2
Signalling type: Colour light
Constructed by: SECR
Year opened: 1856

Services: Passenger
Type of traction: EMU
Electrified: Yes

Bearing off the Tattenham Corner branch at the Chipstead line junction near Purley is the 4.71-mile double tracked line to Caterham, which has three intermediate stations, all with side platforms. A half-hourly service is provided on this line, trains travelling between London and Purley in harness with the Tattenham Corner services. A four-car train led by 2EPB No 5682 arrives at Purley from the Caterham branch in mid-1982. *Colin J. Marsden*

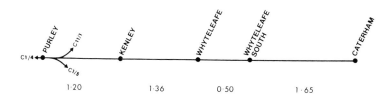

Route: C13
REDHILL-GUILDFORD

Section: C13/1 Redhill-Guildford

Number of lines: 2
Signalling type: Semaphore, Colour light
Constructed by: SECR
Year opened: 1849
Services: Passenger, freight

Types of traction: DMU, EMU, Loco-hauled
Electrified: No*
Notes: *Electrified between Redhill and Reigate.

At the country end of Redhill station the twin tracked cross-country line to Guildford branches off to the right. Although this route is predominantly non-electrified the first 1.84 miles to Reigate is equipped with a third rail. The twin non-electrified tracks then continue with no divergencies past six intermediate stations to Shalford Junction where the route joins into the main Guildford-Portsmouth line, 1.19 miles on the country side of Guildford station. Services over this route are operated by WR DMMU stock and provide an hourly stopping service and an hourly limited-stop service connecting Gatwick Airport with Reading. Freight traffic mainly in the form of engineering trains also traverse the route. WR DMMU set No L579 stops at Deepdene on 17 April 1982 bound for Tonbridge. *Colin J. Marsden*

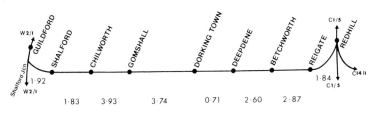

79

Route: C14
REDHILL-TONBRIDGE

Section: C14/1 Redhill-Tonbridge

Number of lines: 2

Signalling type: Semaphore, Colour light

Constructed by: SECR

Year opened: 1842

Services: Passenger, freight

Types of traction: DMU, Loco-hauled

Electrified: No

Veering to the left at the country end of Redhill is the cross-country link to Tonbridge which is 19.70-miles in length and has five intermediate stations, all with side platforms. Apart from a small siding near Godstone the first notable feature on the route is between Leigh and Tonbridge where a connection exists into Tonbridge West yard. Just prior to Tonbridge Station the main SED line from Sevenoaks joins in. This cross-country line is operated by WR DMMUs providing an hourly service to and from Reading. Unit No L581 departs from Redhill and heads for Nutfield during the winter of 1982. *Colin J. Marsden*

Route: C15
THREE BRIDGES-HORSHAM

Section: C15/1 Three Bridges-Horsham

Number of lines: 2
Signalling type: Colour light
Constructed by: LBSCR
Year opened: 1848
Services: Passenger
Type of traction: EMU
Electrified: Yes
Notes: Occasional freight/departmental traffic.

Diverging at the country end of Three Bridges station is the twin tracked route to Horsham and eventually Arundel. The section as far as Horsham is 9.44 miles in length and serves four intermediate stations at Crawley, Ifield, Faygate and Littlehaven. There are no intermediate junctions on the route and the passenger service is operated by EMUs, giving a basic two trains per hour service. Passing the now closed platforms of the original Crawley station and braking for the present station 4CIG No 7370 heads for London with a Littlehampton-Victoria train. *Colin J. Marsden*

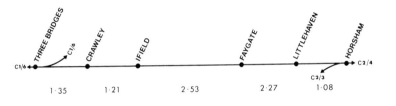

81

Route: C16
WIVELSFIELD-LEWES

Section: C16/1 Wivelsfield-Lewes

Number of lines: 2
Signalling type: Colour light
Constructed by: LBSCR
Year opened: 1847

Services: Passenger
Type of traction: EMU
Electrified: Yes

At Keymer Junction, the country side of Wivelsfield station, the route to Lewes and thence Eastbourne diverges to the left. The 9.27 miles to Lewes is quite uneventful with no special features. At Lewes station the 'Coastway' line from Brighton joins in with separate platform facilities. The line is usually host to only EMU passenger trains but occasional freight traffic does traverse the route. Leaving the Lewes line at Keymer Junction 4CIG No 7332 leads an eight-car formation on an Eastbourne-Victoria diagram. *Colin J. Marsden*

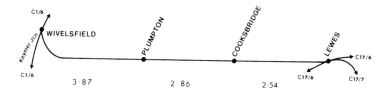

82

Route: C17
HAVANT-
ST LEONARDS & BRANCHES

Section: C17/1 Havant-Chichester

Number of lines: 2
Signalling type: Colour light, semaphore
Constructed by: LBSCR
Year opened: 1847

Services: Passenger, freight
Types of traction: EMU, Loco-hauled
Electrified: Yes

In recent years the route from Portsmouth to Brighton and Ore, has been deemed as the 'Coastway line'. From Portsmouth to Havant the route traverses the same tracks as the Waterloo-Portsmouth services, but at the London end of Havant station the 'Coastway' line continues straight whereas the Waterloo line bears left. The line is of the twin tracked type with on average stations being approximately a mile apart. After departing from Havant the route passes six intermediate stations before reaching Fishbourne crossing near Chichester, where the 2.49-mile Lavant stone branch veers inland. Services over the 'Coastway' line are usually confined to EMU passenger services with some locomotive-hauled freight/departmental trains. 4CIG No 7311 approaches Havant with a Victoria-Portsmouth Harbour via Brighton service. *Colin J. Marsden*

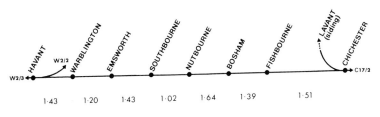

CHICHESTER-LAVANT 2·49

Route: C17
HAVANT-
ST LEONARDS & BRANCHES

Section: C17/2 Chichester-Angmering including Bognor Regis and Littlehampton Branches

Number of lines: 2
Signalling type: Colour light, semaphore
Constructed by: LBSCR
Year opened: 1846
Services: Passenger, freight
Types of traction: EMU, Loco-hauled
Electrified: Yes

This section covers the 'Coastway line' between Chichester and Angmering, as well as the Bognor Regis and Littlehampton branches. The main route is of two tracks, with the Bognor Regis line diverging at Barnham, the next station being Ford where, at the east end of the station the branch to Littlehampton spurs right. Shortly after, Arundel Junction is encountered, where there is a connection with the Mid-Sussex line to Horsham. A facing connection also exists linking the 'Coastway' and Littlehampton line in an east-west direction at Arundel Junction. The Littlehampton branch is also twin tracked with a small EMU stabling point at the terminus. Near Chichester there are three privately owned sidings which generate a small amount of locomotive-hauled traffic. The route usually hosts an endless procession of EMUs except for a few inter-regional services from Brighton to the WR. A 'Coastway' service from Portsmouth approaches Barnham in this view, the line to Bognor diverging to the left under the semaphore signal. *Colin J. Marsden*

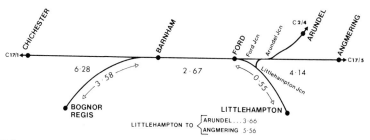

Top:
A HAP-VEP combination arrives at Littlehampton during August 1979 with the 13.52 'Coastway' service from Brighton. On the left is the carriage washing machine, with the depot buildings in the background. HAP type stock no longer operates on this route, all services being in the hands of VEP/CIG type stock. *Les Bertram*

Above:
Occasionally special trains operate along the 'Coastway' line. On 27 August 1979 Class 33 Nos 33.035/063 approach Angmering with a special from the south coast to Yarmouth. *Colin J. Marsden*

Route: C17
HAVANT-
ST LEONARDS & BRANCHES

Section: C17/3 Angmering-Brighton

Number of lines: 2

Services: Passenger, freight

Signalling type: Colour light, semaphore

Types of traction: EMU, Loco-hauled

Constructed by: LBSCR

Electrified: Yes

Year opened: 1846

The 'Coastway' service between Angmering and Brighton is only 15.55 miles in length but has no less than 12 intermediate stations, being on average no more than 1.2 miles apart. The line is all twin tracked with no major divergencies. A small EMU stabling depot is located at West Worthing, and adjacent to Hove a small coal depot is to be found. At the Brighton end of the route a left spur near Hove connects to the main CD Brighton line at Preston Park. Services over this route consist of local 'Coastway' trains to such coastal resorts as Littlehampton, Bognor and Portsmouth, as well as through London services. A small amount of freight/departmental traffic also traverses the route as do a few locomotive-hauled inter-regional services. 4CIG No 7304 approaches Goring-by-Sea on 4 July 1984 with the 11.15 Littlehampton-Victoria service. *John Vaughan*

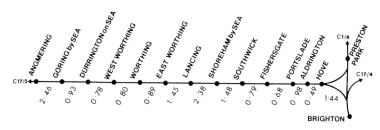

Route: C17
HAVANT-
ST LEONARDS & BRANCHES

Section: C17/4 Brighton-Eastbourne

Number of lines: 2
Signalling type: Colour light, semaphore
Constructed by: LBSCR
Year opened:
1846 to Polegate,
1849 to Eastbourne
Services: Passenger
Types of traction:
EMU, Loco-hauled
Electrified: Yes
Notes: Occasional freight/departmental traffic.

The east 'Coastway' line departs from Brighton and bears sharp right crossing the famous Brighton viaduct before reaching London Road station. The line is of twin track layout and passes through Moulsecoomb and Falmer stations before reaching Lewes where, in the station area the line from Wivelsfield joins in on the left. After departing from Lewes the route travels 1.21 miles to Southerham Junction where the branch to Seaford bears right, the line to Eastbourne continuing as a double track route with four intermediate stops. 0.47 miles before reaching Hampden Park the line passes Willingdon Junction where the route from Hastings and Ore converges. This line is usually host to a constant stream of EMUs with just a few loco operated freight/departmental services. This general view of Eastbourne station shows an 8CIG formation standing in one of the four available platforms. *Colin J. Marsden*

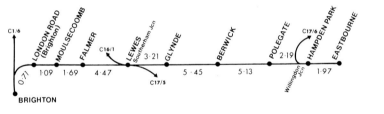

Route: C17
HAVANT-
ST LEONARDS & BRANCHES

Section: C17/5 Lewes-Seaford

Number of lines: 2
Signalling type: Colour light, semaphore
Constructed by: LBSCR
Year opened:
1847 to Newhaven,
1864 Newhaven-Seaford
Services: Passenger
Type of traction: EMU
Electrified: Yes
Notes: Occasional freight/departmental traffic.

Considered as part of the 'Coastway' route is the 7.46-mile branch from Southerham Junction to Seaford. The line is twin tracked as far as Newhaven Harbour from where it is single line on to Seaford. There are two private sidings adjacent to Newhaven Town station, one for car traffic and the other for aggregate; these do, of course, generate a small amount of locomotive-hauled traffic to this otherwise EMU domain. Near Newhaven Town a short 0.28-mile branch to Newhaven Marine spurs off the main route. With both 'up' and 'down' signals being in the 'off' position a four-car formation of HAP stock leaves Bishopstone bound for Seaford.
Brian Morrison

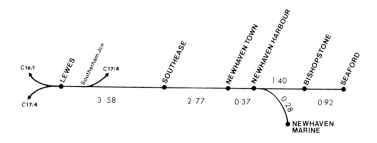

Route: C17
HAVANT-
ST LEONARDS & BRANCHES

Section: C17/6 Hampden Park-St Leonards
Number of lines: 2
Signalling type: Colour light, semaphore
Constructed by: LBSCR
Year opened: 1846
Services: Passenger
Types of traction: EMU, Loco-hauled
Electrified: Yes
Notes: Occasional freight/departmental traffic.

The final part of the 'Coastway' route concerns the 12.42-mile section from Hampden Park to St Leonards Warrior Square. This twin tracked route bears sharp right at Willingdon Junction, with all intermediate stations having side platforms. The line has few significant features except for Galley Hill sidings near Bexhill which see occasional oil traffic, and St Leonards depot, situated between Bexhill and St Leonards Warrior Square being the home for a number of DEMU sets. Just after St Leonards depot is Bopeep Junction where the SED Hastings line converges from the left, the line continuing through Bopeep Tunnel before reaching St Leonards Warrior Square station. Services over this route are usually confined to 'Coastway' duties which are augmented between Bopeep Junction and St Leonards by the hourly DEMU service between London and Hastings. 4CIG No 7311 approaches Normans Bay with an Eastbourne-Ore train. *Colin J. Marsden*

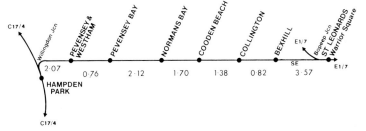

Route: E1
CHARING CROSS/
CANNON STREET-HASTINGS

Section: E1/1 Charing Cross/Cannon Street-London Bridge

Number of lines: 4
Signalling type: Colour light
Constructed by: SER
Year opened: 1864 Charing Cross-London Bridge, 1866 Cannon Street-London Bridge
Services: Passenger
Types of traction: EMU, DMU
Electrified: Yes

The two main London terminals of the South Eastern Division are covered in this section. The station at Charing Cross with its six platforms feeds a four track layout, two up/two down, outside the station, and continues across Hungerford Bridge to Waterloo East, where each line has platform facilities. The route then continues to Metropolitan Junction where an emergency spur converges from the Holborn Viaduct line, and a facing connection is provided to the left with the Cannon Street line. A short distance further on lays Borough Market Junction where the route from Cannon Street joins in. After a further 0.24 miles London Bridge station is reached which has six through lines, five of which have platform facilities. In this general view of Charing Cross station EMU's of Classes 411 and 415 can be seen.
Brian Morrison

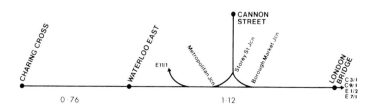

CANNON STREET - LONDON BRIDGE 0·71

90

Route: E1
CHARING CROSS-HASTINGS

Section: E1/2 London Bridge-Hither Green

Number of lines: 4*
Signalling type: Colour light
Constructed by: SER
Year opened: 1865
Services: Passenger, freight
Types of traction: EMU, DMU, Loco-hauled

Electrified: Yes
Notes: *In the area of London Bridge station there are seven running lines a number of which are reversible.

The 5.78 miles from London Bridge to Hither Green is another complex network which is best explained by reference to the map below. Between London Bridge and North Kent East Junction there are seven running lines, some reversible. At North Kent East Junction the twin tracked Deptford route diverges left whilst the now five track main line continues to New Cross where, on the left, there is a platform operated by the LRT Metropolitan line. At the country end of New Cross the SED main line takes a four track configuration to St Johns where the main route bears right and the North Kent line to Lewisham carries straight on. The main line continues to Hither Green while junctions at Lewisham provide connections with the Mid Kent line and the route to Nunhead via Lewisham flyover. A spur also links Lewisham with the Hither Green line at Lewisham Loop Junction. A general view looking south from London Bridge shows a 10EPB formation approaching the station on the 'up No 6' line with a Dartford-Charing Cross via Greenwich service. *Colin J. Marsden*

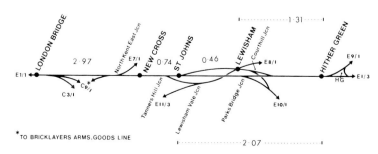

Route: E1
CHARING CROSS-HASTINGS

Section: E1/3 Hither Green-Orpington (including Bromley North branch)

Number of lines: 4
Signalling type: Colour light
Constructed by: SECR
Year opened:
1865 to Chislehurst,
1868 to Orpington
Services: Passenger, freight
Types of traction: EMU, DMU, Loco-hauled
Electrified: Yes

Situated in Hither Green station is the junction taking the Dartford loop line away to the left, while the main route of four tracks continues south, the station having platforms on all lines. At the country end of Hither Green station there is a diesel depot, and a spur connection converges from the Lee line. The main four track route is supplemented from this point to Grove Park by additional lines on both the up and down sides, these being part of Hither Green depot and the Continental terminal. On the left, prior to Grove Park, is an EMU stabling depot which houses a number of units used during peak periods. Grove Park also has platform facilities on all lines and in addition has an 'up loop', which is fed directly from the Bromley North branch diverging right at the country end of the station. The quadruple main continues on through Elmstead Woods to Chislehurst where, after the station, there are connections with the Chatham line which passes beneath; the four track line then goes on to Orpington via Petts Wood. Orpington station has four platforms served by two side and one island platform. Services over this route are usually formed of EMU and DEMU stock on passenger diagrams, and various locomotive classes on freight duties. 4EPB No 5048 departs from Petts Wood with a Charing Cross-Orpington duty. *Colin J. Marsden*

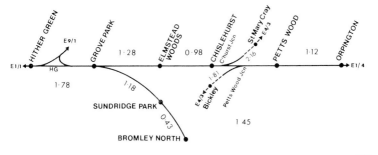

Route: E1
CHARING CROSS-HASTINGS

Section: E1/4 Orpington-Tonbridge

Number of lines: 2
Signalling type: Colour light
Constructed by: SECR
Year opened: 1868
Services: Passenger, freight
Types of traction: EMU, DMU, Loco-hauled
Electrified: Yes

From the country end of Orpington station the route south has a double track layout passing through Chelsfield, Knockholt and Dunton Green before reaching Sevenoaks where, at the London end of the station, the line from Otford joins. The immediate station area at Sevenoaks has four tracks with platform facilities on all lines. The twin route then continues to Tonbridge via Hildenborough. At the London end of Tonbridge station the Redhill line converges from the right adjacent to the west yard. The station itself has two through roads which do not have platforms, these being provided on additional running lines. There is also an up 'loop' and a down bay provided. Services over this section consist of main line passenger trains formed of EMU and DEMU stock which are punctuated by loco operated freight services. Passing Chelsfield a Hastings-Charing Cross train heads for the capital on 4 June 1982 formed of '6S' unit No 1001. *Colin J. Marsden*

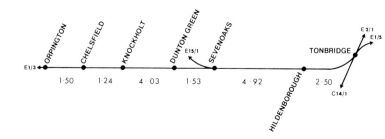

Route: E1
CHARING CROSS-HASTINGS

Section: E1/5 Tonbridge-Wadhurst

Number of lines: 2
Signalling type: Colour light, semaphore
Constructed by: SECR
Year opened: 1852

Services: Passenger
Type of traction: DMU
Electrified: No
Notes: Occasional freight/departmental traffic.

At the country end of Tonbridge station the main electrified route to Ashford continues as the straight route, while the non-electrified line to Hastings branches right and being of the twin tracked style. The first major feature on the route is at Grove Junction, the country side of Tunbridge Wells Central station, where the branch to Tunbridge Wells West and Eridge diverged to the right. The double tracked route then continues to Wadhurst, with one intermediate station at Frant. Services over this section are usually confined to London-Hastings passenger services which basically operate on an hourly diagram with additional trains operating during peak periods. This illustration shows the lovely Frant station which opened in 1851; alterations were carried out in 1859 and the canopy was added in 1904. The line from Grove Junction to Eridge closed in July 1985. *Colin J. Marsden*

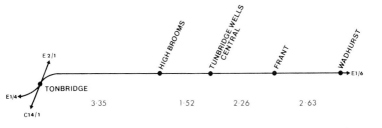

Route: E1
CHARING CROSS-HASTINGS

Section: E1/6 Wadhurst-Hastings

Number of lines: 2
Signalling type: Colour light, semaphore
Constructed by: SECR
Year opened: 1852

Services: Passenger
Type of traction: DEMU
Electrified: No
Notes: Occasional freight/departmental traffic.

One interesting feature of the Hastings line is that a number of stations have semi or staggered platforms. From Wadhurst the route continues through East Sussex passing Stonegate, Etchingham and Robertsbridge stations to Mountfield where due to restricted clearances only a single bore tunnel is provided with a single line controlled by a tokenless block system. A short distance after the tunnel is Mountfield sidings where a gypsum mine owned by British Gypsum Ltd is situated; products from this site are transported by block train to Northfleet cement works. The twin Hastings line then continue through Battle and Crowhurst to West St Leonards where, directly after the station there is Bopeep Junction where the 'Coastway' electrified line from Eastbourne joins. The now electrified route continues on to St Leonards Warrior Square and Hastings where there are two island platforms and four running lines. Standing at Battle station a 12-car formation of 'Hastings' stoc forms a down service in 1982. *Colin J. Marsden*

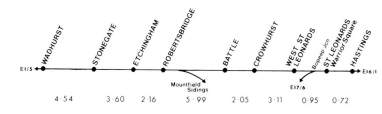

Route: E2
TONBRIDGE-MARGATE
(via DOVER)

Section: E2/1 Tonbridge-Ashford

Number of lines: 2
Signalling type: Colour light
Constructed by: SECR
Year opened: 1842
Services: Passenger, freight
Types of traction: EMU, loco-hauled
Electrified: Yes

The straight route from Tonbridge to Dover is electrified and the first station is Paddock Wood where platform loop lines are provided on both the up and down side. At the country end of the station the line to Maidstone West diverges left, while the main twin track route continues to Ashford via Marden, Staplehurst, Headcorn and Pluckley; all have side platforms except Headcorn which has up/down loops. 3.50 miles after Pluckley is Chart Leacon where on the right side lays a sizeable EMU depot and BR operated works, additional operating lines running from this point to Ashford. Shortly after Chart Leacon the line from Maidstone East joins in from the left. Ashford station has two island platforms served by the slow and additional loop lines, the main lines passing through the middle and being non-platformed. Services over this route are usually of the EMU type with occasional freight traffic. Chart Leacon depot receives a number of SWD/CD EMU types for maintenance, adding to the motive power variety in the area. An 8VEP formation led by unit No 7869 departs from Paddock Wood with an Ashford-Charing Cross train. *Colin J. Marsden*

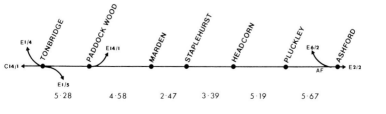

Route: E2
TONBRIDGE-MARGATE
(via DOVER)

Section: E2/2 Ashford-Dover

Number of lines: 2
Signalling type: Colour light
Constructed by: SECR
Year opened: 1844

Services: Passenger, freight
Types of traction: EMU, Loco-hauled
Electrified: Yes

After departing from Ashford the four track configuration continues a short distance, with the Hastings branch diverging on the right, and the route to Canterbury to the left. The SED main, now of two tracks, continues serving Westenhanger and Sandling before reaching Cheriton Junction where additional slow tracks are provided as far as Folkestone Central; platform facilities at Folkestone West and Central are on slow lines only. The two tracked route then goes forward passing the now closed Folkestone East and the Staff Halt at Folkestone Warren, through Shakespeare tunnel and on to Archcliffe Junction, where the straight route continues into Dover Western Docks, or the left divergence goes to Dover Priory. There is also a connection between Dover Priory and Dover Western Docks via Hawkersbury Street Junction. Departing from the 100yd Sandling tunnel and heading for Westenhanger a 12-car EMU led by Class 411 No 1536 forms a Margate-Charing Cross train during 1982. *Colin J. Marsden*

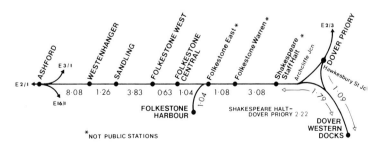

Route: E2
TONBRIDGE-MARGATE
(via DOVER)

Section: E2/4 Sandwich-Margate

Number of lines: 2
Signalling type: Colour light
Constructed by: SER
Year opened: 1847
Services: Passenger

Type of traction: EMU
Electrified: Yes
Notes: Occasional
freight/departmental traffic.

After departing from Sandwich the twin tracked route continues to Minster South Junction where a facing connection with the Minster and Canterbury West line exists. After a further 0.28 miles Minster East Junction is reached where a connection from the Minster, Canterbury line converges. After a further 3.44 miles Ramsgate is reached, where there is a sizeable EMU depot adjacent to the station, Ramsgate itself having four platform lines with sidings on both sides of the station. Onwards from Ramsgate the double track continues through Dumpton Park, which has an island platform, and Broadstairs, which has side platforms, before reaching Margate, having four through platforms and a bay. An unrefurbished 4CEP No 7159 awaits its next turn of duty at Ramsgate depot during 1979. *Colin J. Marsden*

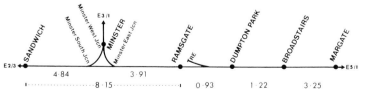

Route: E3
ASHFORD-RAMSGATE
(via MINSTER)

Section: E3/1 Ashford-Ramsgate (via Minster)

Number of lines: 2
Signalling type: Semaphore, Colour light
Constructed by: SER
Year opened: 1846

Services: Passenger, freight
Types of traction: EMU, Loco-hauled
Electrified: Yes

Diverging from the main SER route at Ashford is the 26.54-mile line to Ramsgate via Canterbury West. This double tracked route serves side platform stations at Wye, Chilham and Chartham before reaching the largest station on the line – Canterbury West; this station has two platforms with an additional down goods loop. The twin track then continues via the staggered platforms of Sturry past Chislet Colliery sidings to Minster where, just after the station Minster West Junction takes the line either to Ramsgate or Sandwich. Passing under the famous Canterbury West signalbox Class 411 No 1541 forms the 13.55 Margate-Charing Cross train on 15 April 1984. Traffic over this route is usually confined to EMU passenger services and the occasional freight train. *Brian Morrison*

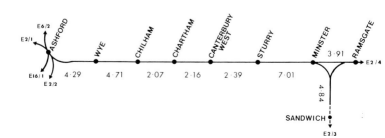

Route: E4
VICTORIA-DOVER

Section: E4/1 Victoria-West Dulwich

Number of lines: 2
Signalling type: Colcur light
Constructed by: LCDR
Year opened: 1862 to Herne Hill,
1863 Herne Hill-West Dulwich
Services: Passenger
Type of traction: EMU
Electrified: Yes

Although Victoria is predominantly a Central Division station, eight of its platforms are designated for SED operation. Shortly after the station the lines take the form of a four track route which, from Battersea Pier Junction to Shepherds Lane, continues as a three track route. After leaving Victoria a left divergence goes to Stewarts Lane depot and freight lines, whilst the main route continues to Factory Junction, where lines from Longhedge Junction and Stewarts Lane converge on the right. Shortly after Factory Junction the SED route runs parallel with the CD South London line which serves stations at Wandsworth Road and Clapham. After passing Clapham station the route to West Dulwich veers right serving Brixton station with its side platforms, before arriving at Herne Hill, a station with two island platforms and four faces. At the London end of Herne Hill the line from Loughborough Junction joins in from the right, whilst at the country end the line to Tulse Hill bears right, the twin tracked main line continuing on to West Dulwich. Traffic over this route consists of main and suburban passenger trains formed of EMU stock and loco-operated freight traffic. 4CAP Nos 3303/3203 approach West Dulwich on 30 November 1984 with the 11.58 Victoria-Maidstone East.
Brian Morrison

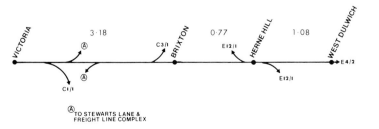

Route: E4
VICTORIA-DOVER

Section: E4/2 West Dulwich-Beckenham Junction

Number of lines: 2
Signalling type: Colour light
Constructed by: LCDR
Year opened: 1863
Services: Passenger, freight
Types of traction: EMU,
Loco-hauled
Electrified: Yes

This short 3.63-mile section of the SED Chatham line between West Dulwich and Beckenham Junction has three intermediate stations. Those at Sydenham Hill and Penge East having side platforms while Kent House has two island platforms and additional loop running lines. The twin tracked route continues to Beckenham Junction where, just before the station, the line from New Beckenham converges on the left, and that from Birkbeck on the right. Beckenham Junction station has two through roads and two bays. Services over this route consist of main line and suburban EMUs and some freight traffic. 4EPB Nos 5217/5009 approach West Dulwich with the 11.25 Orpington-Victoria. Note the Crystal Palace transmitting tower in the background. *Brian Morrison*

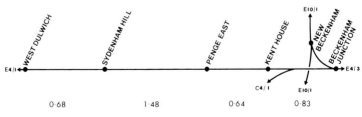

E4/1 ◄━━● WEST DULWICH ━━━━━━━ ● SYDENHAM HILL ━━━━━━━━ ● PENGE EAST ━━━━━━ ● KENT HOUSE ━━━● E4/3

E10/1   NEW BECKENHAM   BECKENHAM JUNCTION

C4/1   E10/1

0·68   1·48   0·64   0·83

NEW BECKENHAM - BECKENHAM JCN 0·55

104

Route: E4
VICTORIA-DOVER

Section: E4/3 Beckenham Junction-Meopham

Number of lines: 2*
Signalling type: Colour light
Constructed by: LCDR
Year opened: 1858 to Bickley,
1860 to Meopham
Services: Passenger,
freight
Types of traction:
EMU, Loco-hauled
Electrified: Yes
Notes: *Four track
Shortlands-Swanley

The twin track route continues 1.15 miles to Shortlands Junction where the line from Nunhead (Catford Loop) joins in from the left, the line then continuing on as a four track route to Swanley. Stations at Shortlands, Bromley South and Bickley have island platforms giving passenger facilities on all tracks. A short distance after Bickley station is Bickley Junction where a right divergence affords a connection with Petts Wood Junction. After a further short distance the route passes under the Chislehurst-Petts Wood line, and St Mary Cray Junction is encountered, where lines link with the Chislehurst-Petts Wood route. The four track Chatham main line continues past St Mary Cray and Swanley, both having island platforms. At the country end of Swanley station the route to Otford bears right and the now twin tracked 'main' line continues to Farningham Road, Longfield and Meopham, all having side platforms. Services over this route are a mixture of main and suburban EMU duties which are punctuated by some freight trains. Class 411 No 1526 passes Bickley station with a Victoria-Ramsgate semi-fast service.
Colin J. Marsden

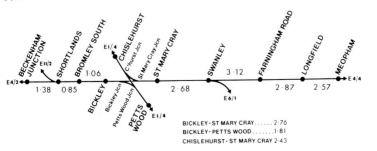

BICKLEY - ST MARY CRAY......2·76
BICKLEY - PETTS WOOD.......1·81
CHISLEHURST - ST MARY CRAY 2·43

Route: E4
VICTORIA-DOVER

Section: E4/4 Meopham-Faversham

Number of lines: 2
Signalling type: Colour light
Constructed by: LCDR
Year opened:
1860 to Rochester,
1858 to Faversham
Services:
Passenger, freight
Types of traction:
EMU, Loco-hauled
Electrified: Yes

This basic twin track section between Meopham and Faversham covers some
26.01 miles and serves 10 stations. The first station on the route is Sole Street
with side platforms. The line then progresses to Rochester Bridge Junction
where a line from Strood joins in on the left, going on to Rochester where
four running lines are located, with two island platforms. Our route then
continues to Chatham where side platforms exist. The next station is
Gillingham where there is an additional reversible line on the 'up' side, with
sidings located on both sides of the line together with a small EMU stabling
point at the country end of the station. The next station is Rainham with side
platforms; the line continues a short distance before additional up and down
loops are provided incorporating Newington station with platforms only on
the loop tracks. The twin configuration continues after Newington station to
Western Junction where a left diversion goes to the Sheerness branch. After
a further short distance Eastern Junction is reached where a down
connection with the Sheerness line is located. Our main route continues
through Sittingbourne and Teynham to Faversham where there are
additional 'up' and 'down' loops in the immediate station area. 4CEP No 7169
stands at Newington with a Victoria-Margate train during 1979.
Colin J. Marsden

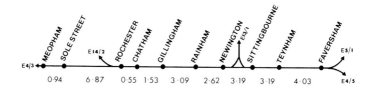

106

Route: E4
VICTORIA-DOVER

Section: E4/5 Faversham-Dover

Number of lines: 2
Signalling type: Colour light
Constructed by: LCDR
Year opened:
1860 to Canterbury,

1861 to Dover
Services: Passenger, freight
Types of traction: EMU,
Loco-hauled
Electrified: Yes

At the country end of Faversham station there is a junction where the lines to Dover and Margate part. This section covers the 25.33 miles to Dover. After passing Faversham Junction the twin track route passes Selling with side platforms and then Canterbury East also having side platforms. Carrying on we pass four further small stations all with side platforms before reaching Snowdown Colliery with sidings to the left. After a further short distance we reach Shepherds Well where the sidings on the left go to Tilmanstone Colliery. The twin track route then passes Kearsney station before reaching Buckland Junction and Dover Priory. This station has one track served by a side platform and an up main and loop line served by an island platform. Services over this route mainly consist of the regular main line passenger duties formed of EMUs, together with a small amount of freight traffic. Class 73 No 73.102 passes Selling with the 15.32 Dundee-Dover ABS on 27 October 1982. *Michael J. Collins*

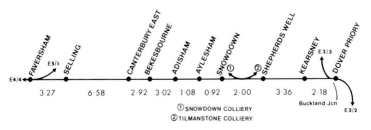

① SNOWDOWN COLLIERY
② TILMANSTONE COLLIERY

Route: E5
FAVERSHAM-MARGATE

Section: E5/1 Faversham-Margate

Number of lines: 2
Signalling type: Colour light
Constructed by: LCDR
Year opened: 1863

Services: Passenger
Type of traction: EMU
Electrified: Yes

The left divergence at the country end of Faversham station leads to Margate via Herne Bay. This is a twin tracked route with five intermediate stations, all having side platforms. No junctions exist on this route. Margate station has additional up and down loop lines in addition to an up facing bay. Services over this section consist of EMU formed passenger trains operating a basic two per hour service; little freight traffic traverses the line. A CEP/VEP/CEP formation led by unit No 1575 departs from Whitstable on 30 May 1982
Brian Morrison

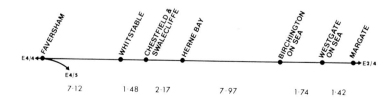

Route: E6
SWANLEY-ASHFORD

Section: E6/1 Swanley-Barming

Number of lines: 2
Signalling type: Colour light
Constructed by: SER
Year opened: 1862 to Otford Junction,
1874 to Barming
Services: Passenger, freight
Types of traction: EMU, Loco-hauled
Electrified: Yes

Diverging from the 'Chatham' main line at Swanley is the twin tracked route to Ashford via Otford and Maidstone. After leaving Swanley the route passes through Eynsford and Shoreham before reaching Otford where, at the country end of the station, our route bears left and the line to Bat & Ball continues straight. The twin tracked Ashford line then continues through Kemsing, Borough Green, West Malling and East Malling to Barming, all stations having side platforms. Trains over this route are mainly the hourly passenger service with occasional freight traffic. 4CEP No 7144 stands at Borough Green & Wrotham station during 1979 with a down service.
Colin J. Marsden

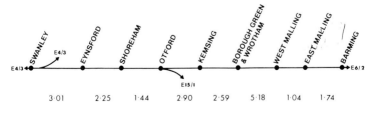

Route: E6
SWANLEY-ASHFORD

Section: E6/2 Barming-Ashford

Number of lines: 2
Signalling type: Colour light, semaphore
Constructed by: LCDR
Year opened: 1874 to Maidstone,
1884 to Ashford
Services: Passenger, freight
Types of traction: EMU, Loco-hauled
Electrified: Yes

This section of 21.67 miles covers the line between Barming and Ashford. After departure from Barming the twin track continues to Maidstone East where an additional up facing bay is located on the down side; there is also a loop line on the up. The route then goes on past Bearstead, Hollingbourne and Harrietsham, all having side platforms, to Lenham where there are sidings on both the up and down sides. There is a down passenger loop the London side of the station and an additional up loop bypasses the station area. The twin track then continues past Charing and Hothfield sidings to Ashford, joining the main SED line near Chart Leacon. 2HAP No 6123 approaches Lenham in 1980 bound for Maidstone East. *Colin J. Marsden*

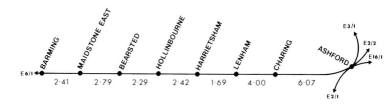

Route: E7
LONDON BRIDGE-ROCHESTER
via WOOLWICH DOCKYARD)

Section: E7/1 London Bridge-Woolwich Dockyard

Number of lines: 2
Signalling type: Colour light
Constructed by: SER
Year opened: See Note 1
Services: Passenger, freight
Types of traction: EMU, Loco-hauled
Electrified: Yes
Notes:
London Bridge-Deptford 1836
Deptford-Greenwich 1838
Greenwich-Maze Hill 1878
Maze Hill-Charlton 1873
Charlton-Woolwich Dockyard 1849

Although this route commences at London Bridge it travels as part of the SED 'main' line to North Kent East Junction, where the twin tracks bear left and head for Deptford, a station with side platforms. The route then continues through Greenwich, Maze Hill and Westcombe Park before reaching Charlton Junction, where the line from Blackheath joins from the right. We then go on through Charlton station with side platforms to Woolwich Dockyard. Between North Kent East Junction and Charlton Junction the route is usually known as the 'Greenwich Line' but from Charlton Junction onwards it is referred to as the 'North Kent Line'. Services over this route normally consist of EMU passenger services punctuated by some loco-operated freight duties. A rare visitor to the line was photographed on 20 January 1979 when two 4TC sets and a Class 73/1 were seen passing Charlton with the 'Electro-Diesel Grice' railtour. *Brian Morrison*

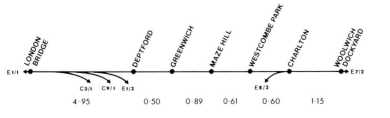

Route: E7
LONDON BRIDGE-ROCHESTER
(via WOOLWICH DOCKYARD)

Section: E7/2 Woolwich Dockyard-Dartford

Number of lines: 2
Signalling type: Colour light
Constructed by: SER
Year opened: 1849
Services:
Passenger, freight
Types of traction:
EMU, Loco-hauled
Electrified: Yes

The 'North Kent' route is of twin track configuration travelling through Woolwich Arsenal, Plumstead, Abbey Wood, Belvedere and Erith before reaching Slade Green, all stations having side platforms. One significant feature is the sidings at the country end of Plumstead station which are used to store damaged SR EMU stock. After Slade Green station there is a right junction forming the Erith loop, giving access to the Bexleyheath line. As the North Kent line progresses it passes the sizeable Slade Green stabling point and maintenance depot, before reaching Crayford Creek Junction where the Bexleyheath line joins from the right. After a further short distance Crayford Spur Junction is reached where a right connection links with the 'Dartford Loop' line, the main route then continuing to Dartford via Dartford Junction. From the Junction to Dartford station an additional reversible running line is provided. Dartford station has four platforms with carriage sidings at the country end on the 'up' side. An 8EPB formation led by set No 5194 pauses at Slade Green station in 1980. *Colin J. Marsden*

Route: E7
LONDON BRIDGE-ROCHESTER
(via WOOLWICH DOCKYARD)

Section: E7/3 Dartford-Rochester

Number of lines: 2
Signalling type: Colour light
Constructed by: SER
Year opened: 1849 to
Gravesend,
1847 to Rochester
Services: Passenger, freight
Types of traction: EMU,
Loco-hauled
Electrified: Yes

After departing from Dartford the double tracked 'main' line passes through Stone Crossing, Greenhithe and Swanscombe before reaching a right junction giving access to the large Northfleet APCM complex. The main route continues through Northfleet to Gravesend where there are platform facilities on the loop tracks. After the immediate station area the line continues on to Hoo Junction, where staggered staff platforms exist together with sidings on both sides of the line; at this point the Grain branch diverges left. The route on to Rochester now passes through Higham before reaching Strood where, at the country end of the three-tracked station the route to Rochester bears left and the line to Cuxton continues on as a straight route. Before actually reaching Rochester the line negotiates Rochester Bridge Junction where the Sole Street line converges from the right. Rochester station has four platform lines served by two island platforms. Services over the Dartford-Rochester section are a mixture of EMU passenger and loco-hauled freight services. 4EPB No 5249 departs from Northfleet with a Charing Cross-Gravesend stopping service. *Colin J. Marsden*

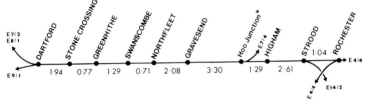

*NOT A PUBLIC STATION

113

Route: E7
LONDON BRIDGE-ROCHESTER
(via WOOLWICH DOCKYARD)

Section: E7/4 Hoo Junction-Grain

Number of lines: Single (Goods line)
Signalling type: Semaphore
Constructed by: SER
Year opened: 1882

Services: Freight only
Types of traction:
Loco-hauled
Electrified: No

Diverging from the Dartford-Gravesend route at Hoo Junction is the 11.43-mile Grain branch serving sidings at Cliffe and Grain. This is a single track line and sees a number of aggregate and oil services each day. Only on very few occasions have passenger trains traversed the line in recent years but on 7 January 1984 a railtour from Plymouth visited the line and is seen here at Cliffe headed by Class 73/1 No 73.107. *Brian Morrison*

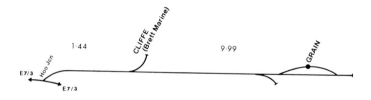

114

Route: E8
LEWISHAM-DARTFORD
(via WELLING)

Section: E8/1 Lewisham-Dartford (via Welling)

Number of lines: 2
Signalling type: Colour light
Constructed by: SER
Year opened:
1849 to Blackheath,
1895 to Dartford
Services: Passenger, freight
Types of traction: EMU,
Loco-hauled
Electrified: Yes

The 'Bexleyheath Line' to Dartford starts from Lewisham and runs as the 'North Kent Line' as far as Blackheath where the line to Charlton and North Kent bears left and that to Dartford continues straight on passing through seven intermediate stations all having side platforms, before reaching Perry Street fork junction where a left spur joins in with the North Kent line at Slade Green. The Bexleyheath line then continues a short distance to Crayford Creek Junction where it joins in the North Kent line for the remainder of the journey to Dartford (E 7/2). Passing Eltham station (under construction) on 12 October 1984 are 4EPB Nos 5164/5146 forming the 11.32 Dartford-Charing Cross working. *Brian Morrison*

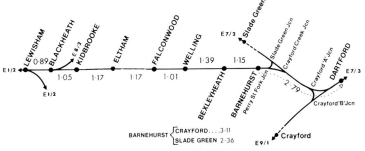

Route: E8
LEWISHAM-DARTFORD

Section: E8/2 Blackheath-Charlton including Angerstein Wharf Branch

Number of lines: 2
Signalling type: Colour light
Constructed by: SER
Year opened: 1849

Services: Passenger
Type of traction: EMU
Electrified: Yes

This short 1.94-mile section joining Blackheath with Charlton and forming part of the 'North Kent Line' is in a tunnel for most of its length. The line bears left just after Blackheath station at Blackheath Junction and joins in with the Westcombe Park-Charlton line at Charlton Junction. Just prior to this junction is Angerstein Junction where a freight only branch to Angerstein Wharf diverges; this is a freight only line serving two stone terminals and a metal scrapyard. A train of Class 411 stock approaches Charlton Junction in December 1984. Note the Angerstein Wharf line diverging to the right at the rear of the train. *Brian Morrison*

ANGERSTEIN WHARF

BLACKHEATH
Blackheath Jcn

Angerstein Wharf Jcn
E7/1
Charlton Jcn
CHARLTON

E8/1

E8/1

1·94

E7/1

ANGERSTEIN:JUNCTION TO WHARF 1·04

HITHER GREEN-DARTFORD

Section: **E9/1 Hither Green-Dartford**

Number of lines: 2
Signalling type: Colour light
Constructed by: SER
Year opened: 1866

Services: Passenger, freight
Types of traction: EMU, Loco-hauled
Electrified: Yes

Diverging from the SE main line at Hither Green and running the 9.98 miles to Dartford is the 'Dartford Loop' line; shortly after Hither Green station the Lee spur joins in on the right, giving a non-passenger connection with the SED main line. The double tracked 'Dartford Loop' continues through seven intermediate stations all with side platforms before reaching Crayford Spur Junction where a left lead connects with the 'North Kent' line in an 'up' direction. The 'Dartford Loop' joins in the 'North Kent' route at Dartford Junction and forms part of the three line configuration into Dartford station. Trains over this route are provided at 30min intervals and a number of freight trains are also users of the line. 4EPB No 5194 stops at New Eltham with a Dartford-Charing Cross train in 1982. *Colin J. Marsden*

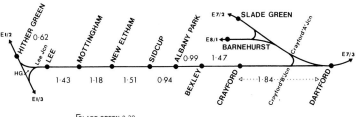

Route: E10
LEWISHAM-HAYES/ADDISCOMB[

Section: E10/1 Lewisham-Hayes

Number of lines: 2
Signalling type: Colour light
Constructed by: SER
Year opened:
1857 to New
Beckenham,
1864 to Elmers End,
1882 to Hayes
Services: Passenger
Type of traction: EMU
Electrified: Yes

At the country end of Lewisham station the right divergence leads to
Courthill Loop North Junction where a right spur leads to Ladywell Junction
and thence Ladywell station. This twin tracked route leads to Hayes passing
through Catford Bridge and Lower Sydenham before reaching New
Beckenham where, at the country end of the station a left spur leads to
Beckenham Junction. The main route continues via Clock House to Elmers
End where, after the station, at Elmers End Junction our route to Hayes via
Eden Park and West Wickham spurs left and the line to Addiscombe
continues straight on. All stations on the route have side platforms and
Elmers End has an additional bay. Passenger services over the line operate at
30min intervals. EPB No 5143 leads the 11.24 Hayes-Cannon Street service
under the SED main line towards the Lewisham stop on 3 January 1984.
Brian Morrison

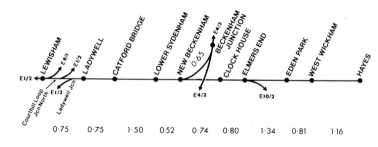

Section: E10/2 Elmers End-Addiscombe

Number of lines: 2
Signalling type: Colour light
Constructed by: SER
Year opened: 1864

Services: Passenger
Type of traction: EMU
Electrified: Yes

The short 1.87-mile branch between Elmers End and Addiscombe is a twin track route serving one intermediate station at Woodside. A small EMU stabling depot is located near Addiscombe and trains on the line are confined to passenger services operating at 30min intervals, normally as a shuttle to and from Elmers End. 2EPB No 5770 stands at Addiscombe on 20 January 1979 with a shuttle for Elmers End. *Brian Morrison*

Route: E11
PECKHAM RYE-SHORTLANDS/
LEWISHAM

Section: E11/1 Peckham Rye-Shortlands

Number of lines: 2
Signalling type: Colour light
Constructed by: LCDR
Year opened: 1892

Services: Passenger
Type of traction: EMU
Electrified: Yes

Shortly after Peckham Rye station the SED tracks cross the CD SLL and head
for Nunhead and the Catford Loop Line. At the country end of Nunhead
station which has an island platform, a left junction takes the twin track to
Lewisham. The Catford Loop continues via Crofton Park, Catford,
Bellingham, Beckenham Hill and Ravensbourne to Shortlands where, at the
London end of the station, the twin track from Beckenham joins in, making a
four tracked route into Shortlands station. Services over the line mainly
consist of EMU passenger services and occasional freight trains. EPB units
Nos 5041/5119 depart from Crofton Park with a Sevenoaks bound train in late
1984. *Brian Morrison*

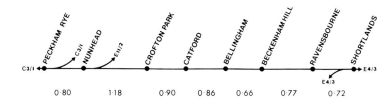

Section: E11/2 Nunhead-Lewisham

Number of lines: 2

Signalling type: Colour light

Constructed by: LCDR

Year opened: 1892

Services: Passenger, freight

Types of traction: EMU, Loco-hauled

Electrified: Yes

This short 1.83-mile connecting line between Nunhead and Lewisham is an important 'link' connection for the SR and apart from being traversed by regular passenger trains sees a sizeable amount of freight traffic. After leaving Nunhead the line to Shortlands branches to the right at Nunhead Junction with the twin tracked route going on to Lewisham Vale Junction and thence Lewisham. Class 47 No 47.110 passes through Nunhead station with an up airbraked freight service in December 1984. *Brian Morrison*

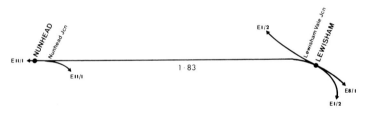

121

Route: E12
HOLBORN VIADUCT-TULSE HILL
Section: E12/1 Holborn Viaduct-Tulse Hill
Number of lines: 2
Signalling type: Colour light
Constructed by: LCDR/LBSCR
Year opened:
1862 to Herne Hill,
1868 to Tulse Hill
Services: Passenger, freight
Types of traction: EMU,
Loco-hauled
Electrified: Yes

Holborn Viaduct is a three platformed terminal station which feeds into a twin route outside the station for a distance of 0.38 miles to Blackfriars, where the station has three further bay platforms. After the station area a four tracked route is formed and a short distance further on at Blackfriars Junction a left spur is made with Metropolitan Junction the four track route continuing through Elephant & Castle which has an island and two side platforms, to Loughborough Junction where, just prior to the station a twin track spur diverges left to Cambria Junction and another bears right to Canterbury Road Junction; the now two tracked route to Herne Hill feeding an island platform at Loughborough Junction. A short distance after Loughborough Junction station the route approaches Herne Hill North Junction where the two tracked line from Brixton joins in from the right. Herne Hill station has two island platforms and four tracks, and at the countr end of the station the twin tracked Beckenham line veers left and our route now also of two tracks bears right and shortly reaches Tulse Hill where, just prior to the four tracked station the line from Peckham Rye joins from the left Services over this route are mainly of EMU passenger formations with a few freight trains intermingled. 4EPB No 5112 stands at Elephant & Castle with a Wimbledon bound service in 1984. *Colin J. Marsden*

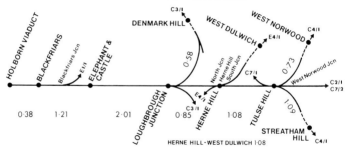

Route: E13
SITTINGBOURNE-
SHEERNESS-ON-SEA

Section: E13/1 Sittingbourne-Sheerness-on-Sea

Number of lines: See Notes
Signalling type: Colour light
Constructed by: LCDR
Year opened: 1860
Services: Passenger, freight
Types of traction: EMU,

Loco-hauled
Electrified: Yes
Notes: Double –
Sittingbourne-Swale.
Single – Swale-Sheerness.

Diverging from the Rochester-Faversham line at Western and Eastern
Junctions near Sittingbourne are up/down facing connections on to the
Sheerness branch. This line is of double track layout as far as Swale and
single track forward to Sheerness with a passing place at Queenborough.
Apart from the regular EMU shuttle service between Sittingbourne and
Sheerness and rush-hour through trains to and from London, the line sees a
fair amount of freight traffic as there are sizeable freight complexes at
Ridham Dock, Queenborough and Sheerness. Class 411 No 1529 stands at
Sheerness, which has two side platforms and an electrified centre siding.
Colin J. Marsden

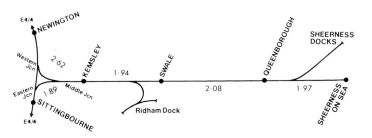

123

Route: E14
PADDOCK WOOD-STROOD

Section: E14/1 Paddock Wood-Maidstone Barracks

Number of lines: 2
Signalling type: Semaphore, Colour light
Constructed by: SER
Year opened: 1844

Services: Passenger, freigh
Types of traction: EMU, Loco-hauled
Electrified: Yes

Diverging to the left at the country end of Paddock Wood station is the branc
to Strood via Maidstone. After leaving Paddock Wood a *Transfesa* terminal
lays on the left which generates a small amount of freight traffic. The twin
track continues on through five intermediate stations before reaching
Maidstone Barracks all of which have side platforms; Maidstone West has ar
additional centre up main line, and Maidstone Barracks has sidings adjacent
to the station. Services are mainly confined to the Paddock Wood-Strood
shuttle which operates on an hourly basis; some freight traffic also uses the
line. 4EPB No 5262 stands at Beltring heading for Paddock Wood.
Colin J. Marsden

E2/1   PADDOCK WOOD   1·85   BELTRING   1·61   YALDING   1·73   WATERINGBURY   2·97   EAST FARLEIGH   1·83   MAIDSTONE WEST   0·43   MAIDSTONE BARRACKS   E14/2

E2/1

PADDOCK WOOD-STROOD

Section: **E14/2 Maidstone Barracks-Strood**

Number of lines: 2
Signalling type: Colour light, semaphore
Constructed by: SER
Year opened: 1856

Services: Passenger, freight
Types of traction: EMU, Loco-hauled
Electrified: Yes

The 10.86-mile section between Maidstone Barracks and Strood is twin tracked with five intermediate stations all having side platforms. Between Maidstone Barracks and Aylesford is Allington Roadstone terminal which receives a daily stone train from Westbury. There are also sidings at New Hythe which serve the Reed Paperworks; and between Snodland and Halling there are the Holborough Blue Circle Cement sidings. Just after Halling station the Rugby Cement works are situated on the right which has daily powdered cement traffic. At Strood the line from Higham and the North Kent route joins in. Passenger services are usually two per hour with some freight traffic. 4EPB No 5188 stands at Aylesford during the summer of 1982.
Colin J. Marsden

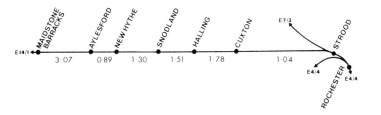

Route: E15
OTFORD-SEVENOAKS

Section: E15/1 Otford-Sevenoaks

Number of lines: 2

Signalling type: Colour light

Constructed by: LCDR

Year opened: 1862

Services: Passenger

Type of traction: EMU

Electrified: Yes

Notes: Occasional freight/departmental traffic.

The 2.77-mile section linking Otford with Sevenoaks is a twin tracked route with one intermediate station at Bat & Ball where, at the country end of the station, there is a small stone terminal operated by the Redland Company. The route is usually traversed by suburban EMUs which provide an hourly service. The stone terminal receives one train daily usually operated by a Class 47 or 56 locomotive. Class 415/1 Nos 5248/5189 approach Bat & Ball on 12 October 1984 with the 14.50 Sevenoaks-Holborn Viaduct, the Redland stone siding diverges to the right. *Brian Morrison*

Route: E16
ASHFORD-HASTINGS

Section: E16/1 Ashford-Hastings and Dungeness Branch

Number of lines: See Note 1
Signalling type: Semaphore, Colour light
Constructed by: SER
Year opened: 1851
Services: Passenger (see Note 2)
Types of traction: DMU, loco-hauled
Electrified: No
Notes: 1: Ashford-Appledore – 2 tracks.
Appledore-Hastings – single (passing place at Rye)
2: Occasional freight traffic on Dungeness branch

The route between Ashford and Hastings is a non-electrified line except for a short distance at the Ashford end and also between Ore and Hastings. The Ore-Hastings section is double tracked with the stations having side platforms, with a small EMU stabling point adjacent to Ore station. From Ore the route is a single line to Appledore with a passing place at Rye. The double track layout continues from Appledore to Ashford; diverging at Appledore is the freight only Dungeness Nuclear Power Station line which sees spasmodic traffic. Ore station is the eastern extremity of the 'Coastway Line' and 4CIG No 7368 was photographed in the station on an eastbound working in 1982.
Colin J. Marsden

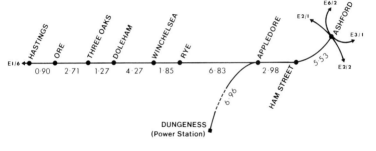

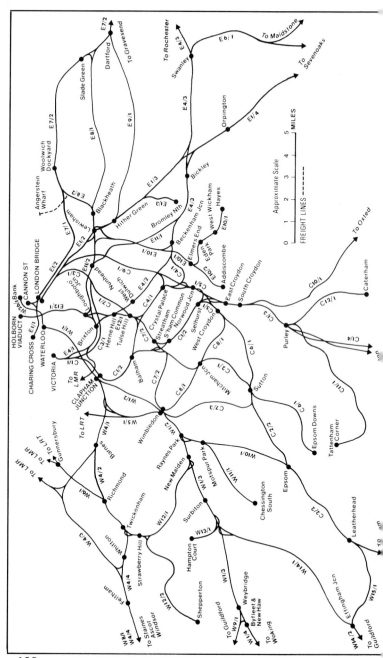

128